THE
SUCCESS
MATRIX

THE
SUCCESS
MATRIX

WINNING IN BUSINESS
AND IN LIFE

GERRY LANGELER

LOGOS
PRESS

THE SUCCESS MATRIX
WINNING IN BUSINESS AND IN LIFE
GERRY LANGELER

Published in The United States of America
by
Logos Press®, Washington, DC
www.Logos-Press.com
info@Logos-Press.com

10 9 8 7 6 5 4 3 2 1

ISBN-13
Softcover: 978-1-934899-19-9

Library of Congress Cataloging-in-Publication Data

Langeler, Gerry.
  The success matrix : winning in business and in life / Gerry
Langeler.
     pages cm
  ISBN 978-1-934899-19-9 (softcover)
  1. Success in business. 2. Success. I. Title.
  HF5386.L2425 2014
  650.1--dc23
                          2013043228

PRAISE FOR *THE SUCCESS MATRIX*

"If you've spent any time at all in the business world, you'll recognize all of the characters Gerry Langeler clearly describes in *The Success Matrix*. And if you haven't spent any time in the business world, then it's all the more important for you to read this book. It's an effective, insightful portrait of the personalities one encounters on a daily basis, and also a spot-on how-to manual for anyone who endeavors to find success, presented by one who's had much experience in doing so."
Bob Lutz, former Vice Chair, General Motors. Author of *Car Guys vs. Bean Counters: The Battle for the Soul of American Business*, and *Icons and Idiots: Straight Talk on Leadership*

"I really liked this book. Gerry Langeler understands from his considerable hands-on experience that blending and empowering a diverse assortment of personalities and skills is the key to any successful enterprise. He provides an easy-to-use approach to identifying key types of people and then employing their particular talents to achieve success in any endeavor."
Steve Wynne, former CEO, Adidas America

"The Success Matrix is an insightful, practical approach to assessing people and organizations, firmly rooted in the author's more than thirty years of experience as an entrepreneur, corporate leader and venture capital funds manager."
Allan Moss, Principal of Allan Moss Investments pty ltd, former CEO of Macquarie Group, Australia

Also by Gerry Langeler

Take the Money and Run! An Insider's Guide to Venture Capital, Lulu Press, 2011, ISBN 978-1-257-86689-2. E-book available at Smashwords.com and all popular e-book sites.

The Vision Trap, Harvard Business Review, April 1992, ISSN Number: 0017-8012.

Chapter: "Patently Ridiculous" in *Great Patents*, Logos Press, 2011, ISBN 978-1-934899-17

Chapter: "Exit, Stage Right" in *Venture Capital Best Practices*, Aspatore Books, 2005, ISBN 1-59622-035-X

Contents

Acknowledgements

Thanks to Professor Rob Wiltbank, who suggested the fictional "bookend" approach I used in chapters one and eleven, and got me working again on the manuscript after it had languished for several years. Thanks as well to my long-time assistant, Linda Hoban, for her support. My editor, Brian Kiernan, took the initial manuscript and added much-needed polish. Finally, I am grateful to my family, who remind me daily that any success I may have in business pales compared to the importance of what waits for me at home.

Foreword

The *Success Matrix: Winning in Business and in Life* takes a slightly different approach than most business books. A typical business book guides the reader through its prescribed methods and tools, using various real world examples to support its concepts and conclusions. In fact, chapters two through ten of *The Success Matrix* do just that.

But *The Success Matrix* is atypical in chapters one and eleven. In those chapters I chose to convey the basic concepts of the book in a format that should be more accessible and recognizable to readers who are themselves executives, managers, entrepreneurs or individual contributors: a fictional account of one executive's exposure to *The Success Matrix*, as explained to him by his friend and mentor. When you have read chapter one, hopefully you not only will have enjoyed this fictional sketch and have a foundation on which the succeeding chapters will build, but you already will find yourself categorizing people you know, or organizations with which you interact, along the lines of some of the story's characters. As you will see, the value of *The Success Matrix* can also extend quite readily to your life outside of business. When you finish chapter eleven, I hope you'll see how you can apply the general principals found in *The Success Matrix* to your specific company, business, department, organization or startup dream.

AUTHOR'S NOTE

All the characters in chapters one and eleven are fictional, with one obvious exception. In that case, her past exploits are well-documented, although her situation in *The Success Matrix* is complete fiction. Any connection or correlation to any other real individual is unintended and coincidental.

ONE

The Interview

Chris Jameson stared at his cell phone for a full three minutes after the call had concluded. He hadn't expected this. After his last set of interviews with the headhunter and the recruiting company's board chair, he wasn't particularly optimistic about his chances. But apparently those meetings had gone better than he thought. It seemed they really valued his startup experience, his youthful enthusiasm, his high tech connections, and the fact that he'd gotten his international ticket punched.

So, the good news was they liked him. And the bad news was they liked someone else as well. He was one of just two finalists. The job of a lifetime, his dream position, was within his reach but not yet his grasp. He was one tantalizing step away from being named CEO of the fastest growing, most visible, and, yes, *sexiest* company he could imagine: Ultramax, the Wall Street darling that had almost single-handedly lifted the entire high technology market out of its doldrums. His assignment (well, not yet his, but close, so close!) would be to lead the enterprise and those very bright folks who had pioneered the energy storage breakthrough in ultracapacitors that finally made electric vehicles practical. It was a global, massive and stunning opportunity ... and he was scared to death. Scared of the final hurdle to the top job that the headhunter had described just before the call ended.

On Monday morning, just three days away, Chris was due in New York. He'd be in a conference room all day with the management team he would inherit if he got the job, while the headhunter, the board chair and the search committee of the board would be watching his every move behind a one-way mirror. Over the course of the day, he would have to demonstrate how he would lead and manage people whom he had never met. Most were older than he was, and certainly some of them might well resent him for being a finalist for a job they had coveted.

The headhunter had made it clear that they were not looking for any particular brilliance on his part about strategy, or market, or even the industry. They wanted to see, and hear, and get a feel for how he would lead and manage an organization. How would he figure out which levers to pull to get the most out of the team? How would he figure out where he needed to add—or subtract—key players? How would he build a culture of sustainable high performance and repeatable results that would maintain Wall Street's enthusiasm?

"Now," Chris thought, "it isn't as if I haven't worked hard to get this opportunity. And my success managing organizations is well documented. But, realistically, this is a big step up for me in complexity and visibility, and all with a team I know almost nothing about. There must be some approach, model, or framework I can use to structure this meeting in a way that will impress the board and engage my soon-to-be (I hope) direct reports."

Chris put down the cell phone and pulled out paper and pencil. Even after years at a keyboard, he found he thought better with a pencil in his hand. His mind focused on some of the business books he had read over the years. Perhaps in them, or one of them, there was a key, maybe *the* key, to getting out of that conference room not just alive but triumphant.

"Let's see," he murmured, "there's Geoff Moore's great book, *Crossing the Chasm.* That's almost a bible for folks in high tech, high growth businesses. But it's really more about product and market strategy than organizational excellence. And his other books mostly enlarged and updated his thinking. Maybe after I'm in the job—how's that for positive thinking!—that will help. But it won't help me on Monday.

"And of course there's Steven Covey with his *Seven Habits of Highly Successful People.* I'm sure everyone in the room will have read Covey. So, let's see, those seven habits were ..." and he paused. "Oh yes, 'Start with the end in mind.' That's one. What are the others?" He racked his brain, and found ... nothing. How could that be? Wasn't Covey the guru of personal and organizational effectiveness? Hadn't he built a publishing empire around those seven habits? And yet here he was, realizing that despite what Covey brought to the table, he hadn't brought lasting, memorable value ... at least not to Chris.

He went through his list more quickly now, "*Built to Last*? Great, but no—all about major corporate behavior.

The World is Flat? Terrific global perspective, but nothing to say about running an enterprise. *Decisive?* Very helpful to improve decision-making, but not for driving organizational balance."

He put down the pencil as though it had betrayed him. It seemed there was no guide available. No book, no model, no concept, no tool. Monday had drawn closer as he wasted precious minutes with his phantom reading list. He walked to the coffee machine, wondering why people were looking at him so strangely. "Do they know? How could they know?" Finally he realized that in his fog after answering the cell phone, he'd forgotten to take off his raincoat. He had been sitting at his desk and scribbling on his paper and now was off to the coffee machine looking like he expected a monsoon to sweep through the building. He laughed with a co-worker. "Guess I've got a lot on my mind this morning." It sounded hollow, but at least it covered his tracks.

Back at his desk, coffee in hand, raincoat on its hook, he pondered a new approach. "There must be someone who can help me put together an approach for Monday with something other than, "Hi, my name is Chris. Let's wing it and hope for the best!"

He thought of his boss and mentor from his first start-up. Henry Long always seemed able to simplify complex issues and provide a way for folks to communicate productively. He'd gone on to be a venture capitalist, helping many young, high growth companies over the years. But, if Chris remembered correctly, he'd retired a few years ago, moved to Vermont, and taken up painting. And wasn't that redundant, he chuckled. A retired venture capitalist?

He sent a plaintive email to Henry, and waited.

THE JOURNEY TO MEMPHREMAGOG

Chris didn't have to wait very long. It was as if Henry had just been waiting to be asked. The response was warm and heartfelt. "I'd be delighted to see you again, and yes, I think I might be able to help a little. Below is a Google Maps link to my humble abode on the shores of Lake Memphremagog. Newport's about an hour and a half drive from the Burlington airport. I'll expect you for dinner tomorrow night, and we'll see what we can figure out over the weekend."

"That's terrific," Chris thought, "but what does 'figure out over the weekend' mean? I'm flying across the country so he can tell me he's already got it all figured it out? Let it be so!"

Chris set about booking a Saturday crack-of-dawn flight cross-country to Vermont.

The flight was uneventful, and even though Chris was anxious to get to Henry's to start finding a solution to his problem, he enjoyed the drive from the airport, winding through the hills of northern New England. Thanks to the GPS app on his iPad, he had no trouble finding Henry's house at the end of a fairly narrow road on a hill overlooking both Lake Memphremagog to the north and the small town of Newport to the east.

Henry must have heard the car crunch on the gravel

driveway: he was standing on the front steps before Chris could get out. "Well hello, stranger!" Henry called. "It's been way too long."

"Yes, it has," said Chris. "I think the last time you gave me some advice, I didn't follow it, and it cost me. This time, I'll pay closer attention."

"You'd better, because the secret I'm going to share with you is known only to me, and I hope someday my publisher, if I ever get around to writing the damn thing down."

They shook hands warmly and Henry led Chris into the house, showed him where the guest bedroom and bath were, and then put some steaks on the outdoor grill and opened one of his more expensive bottles of wine. Chris reappeared a few moments later, and they sat down in the living room. One of the first things he noticed was a very large fish mounted over the fireplace.

"Is that one of those plastic fish that sings?" he asked with a straight face.

"That, my friend," said Henry, "is the mother of all lake trout, caught just this side of the border on that big body of water over your shoulder. If I'd been a few hundred yards farther north, Canadian Customs might have charged me duty on it!"

Chris laughed. It was good to be with his old friend again, and for the first time in two days he felt like he might get real help with his problem. "So, I hate to cut to the chase, but while we're talking fish, we've only got tonight and tomorrow for you to 'school' me on how to handle this interview on Monday." Chris never missed an opportunity for a lousy play on words.

Henry cooperatively groaned at the pun, "Yes, I agree it's not much time. But for tonight, let me just share with you the skeleton of what I plan to give you as an approach. Tomorrow, we'll walk into town and I'll put the meat on the bones. You know that all business success revolves around three basic variables: Vision, Process and Output. Now maybe you haven't thought about it exactly in those terms before, but in reality that's all there is to it.

- Do you have the Vision of where you need to go and what you need to do over time?
- Do you have the skills and techniques, the Process, to do those things reliably and repeatedly?
- Do you have proof that you are doing what you say you need to in the form of high quality Output from your efforts?"

"That's it? That's all? As much as I enjoy your company, Henry, I didn't need to fly 3000 miles for that. You could have told me that over the phone, not that it would be enough to help me on Monday." Chris was trying to be polite, but his disappointment was evident.

Henry was not surprised by the reaction. "It does sound simple doesn't it? Worse, it sounds simplistic. But I'll bet by the time you leave tomorrow you'll have a different opinion. What makes this interesting is when you start to categorize people and organizations against those three variables: whether they have them or they don't. Think quick: you have three variables and two conditions. How many possibilities are there?"

Chris wasn't good at everything, but he was always a whiz at math. "Eight. Two to the third power."

"Right you are," Henry grinned. "Tomorrow, you'll get to understand those eight conditions in very personal terms. I'm going to introduce you to eight real people, let's call them my 'characters,' who are the embodiment of those eight possibilities. Put together, those eight create what I call the Success Matrix. Here, I'll sketch it out for you."

Henry quickly drew a grid eight squares high by three wide on a piece of paper. He labeled the three rows across the top "Vision," "Process" and "Output" and then put an X in the boxes showing all the possible combinations.

It looked like this:

vision	process	output
X		
X	X	
X		X
	X	
	X	X
		X
—	—	—
X	X	X

"If you pay close attention, by the end of the day tomorrow you'll know how to label those eight rows, how to understand what each person represents as a direct report, and understand where your new organization is strong, where it's weak, and where you need to make changes."

"That seems like a tall order for such a simple construct," Chris didn't want to appear ungrateful, but he still was skeptical.

"OK, but reserve judgment until the end of the day tomorrow." Henry seemed energized by the challenge of selling his concept to his young friend. "Until then, let's enjoy the view of the lake and this lovely wine."

THE DAY IN NEWPORT

The next morning Henry was up early, while Chris, still on west coast time, slept in. By the time he came out of the bedroom, Henry had a cup of coffee in his hand and the morning paper in his lap. "Glad to see you're among the living," he chided. "Actually, this is perfect timing. I've had my coffee and read the paper, but held off on breakfast until you rousted yourself. We'll walk down to the local diner. They have the best oatmeal in Vermont. Try it with maple syrup rather than brown sugar. It's fabulous."

After a brisk walk in the cool spring air, they settled into a booth at Millie's. It was one of those classic diners that appeared to be made from a silver mobile home trailer. They placed their orders, and Henry got down to business.

"I'd like to introduce you to Scott Anderson," Henry tilted his head in the direction of a distinguished-looking older man sitting in the corner. They shook hands and

Henry mentioned that Scott was into photography. That led to talk of the latest photo editing software, and Scott started to describe how to make some fascinating artwork by taking color photographs and reducing them to stark black and white, with no halftones. The thought crossed Chris' mind that maybe this Matrix thing Henry had described last night might end up being a little too black and white to be useful.

Henry and Chris went back to their booth. "Scott there may be one of the most creative, innovative people on the planet. On the other hand, he also may be one of the most wasted talents on the planet. Ideas just spark off the guy, like the way he immediately got you discussing creative photography. He's sort of a combination of Walter Mitty and Rube Goldberg, always dreaming up new inventions. Some of them might even have commercial value. But while he was successful in the architectural design business, where conceptual ideas alone often were enough to win the day and he had a staff to implement his ideas, he's failed to get any of his inventions to market."

"What's his problem?" Chris asked.

"He has all sorts of Vision, but just doesn't seem to know how to translate his Vision, with a Process to deliver on it, into real Output. He'll slap together crude prototypes, but then, like a crow, he gets attracted to the next shiny object and he's off on a new quest."

"So he's just a flake, isn't he?" Chris wasn't one to mince words.

"Quite the contrary. He's the first of our 'characters.' I call him a Dreamer. He's an inventor, a creative genius. And we certainly need those. Dreamers are the kind of optimistic folks who get us all fired up to go conquer new territory. They are the explorers. Scott's Vision and creativity could be very powerful if he ever teamed up with some folks who could filter his ideas, pick the best ones, and then execute on them. He did that back in his architecture days. The problem now is that he's retired and doesn't have anyone to implement for him. As it stands, Dreamers by themselves often do end up looking like flakes. And Dreamers are no-toriously hard to pair with the people they need most to become successful. They just don't have the patience. But once in a while, Dreamers do get religion, even if it's only temporary. When they can find a way to stay focused long enough to deliver on their dream, or guide others to, they can change the world."

"I've seen plenty of those folks in the advanced R&D operation at my current company," Chris said. "Most of the time, they act like spoiled children and are extra over-head to boot. No accountability and no schedules: must be a wonderful life."

"That can be true," replied Henry, "But don't ignore the potential of Dreamers. I'll explain later what happens if you do."

"Now, see that guy by the window buried in his newspa-per?" asked Henry. "That's Sanjay Mitra. He's an adjunct professor at Middlebury College, about two hours south of here. He lives in Newport, but has an apartment down there for the days he teaches or holds office hours. Sunday is one of his "off" days.

"What's the story with him?" Chris was already guessing that everyone Henry pointed out was going to have some connection to his quest to understand this "Success Matrix" thing.

"As I said, he's a professor. He's got terrific Vision of the way things should be, and he can describe in great detail from his research what it takes to make those things happen. But that's as far as he takes it. He tells others what their Output should be, but he doesn't take on that heavy lifting himself. He's an Academic."

"Of course he is! He's a professor."

Henry could see Chris's confusion. "No, not an academic—an 'Academic'." He used his fingers to make quote marks in the air. "An Academic has nothing to do with being a professor, even though you'll find many 'Academics' in their ranks. An Academic is someone with Vision and Process but no Output. You remember the old saying, 'Those that can, do. Those that can't, teach?' It goes far beyond the ivy covered walls.

"Think about some of the people you've known in staff positions in your career. They often are very bright, hardworking folks, to be sure. But they also have the luxury of recommending everything without being responsible for the consequences of anything. It may be that they are really good thinkers, but not doers. Being a philosopher is a whole lot easier than being a plumber. Or it may be they are risk averse, and don't want to step out on a limb where Output is the criteria for success. But whatever their motivation, they are all Academics."

"So, that makes them blowhards. I know the type. Cocktail party experts." Chris was thinking about some staffers in his current company who showed up at strategic planning meetings with charts and graphs reflecting the latest management fad, only to seemingly disappear until the following year's meeting.

"Yes, they can be." Henry could see he had more work to do himself as a teacher to get Chris to understand where he was trying to take him. "But they also can be critical to the growth of an organization. Academics can step back and see the forest while all the operating guys are bumping into trees. Academics can help others in your company balance the short term with the long term. Just make sure you don't get so impressed with their intelligence and articulate language that you put them in a position where their Output can determine the success of the enterprise. Many a failed company has put a brilliant staffer, an Academic, in a key line management position and not lived to tell the tale.

"By the way, don't share this dirty little secret, but a lot of venture capitalists are Academics. They are more than happy to tell you what to do, and even how to do it. But when it comes to getting down in the trenches and producing something, they're off to the golf course!"

"Oops, sorry if I inadvertently called you a blowhard!" Chris was embarrassed. "OK, I get the Dreamer and the Academic. What's next?"

"Here comes our food, so I'd say the oatmeal is next." Henry smiled.

The conversation drifted to their personal lives since they'd been together last, along with a little ribbing about whether the Celtics or the Lakers were going to win the NBA championship that year.

Henry suggested they work off breakfast with a stroll to the docks on Lake Memphremagog. It was a lovely day, and Chris was ready for a little break from The Success Matrix. So far, he wasn't sure this was going to provide him that magic methodology he needed for Monday morning. On the way back up the hill, Henry suggested a cappuccino. Chris readily agreed.

As they took their seats at the coffee shop counter, in walked one of the prettiest women Chris had seen in a long time. Henry noticed his eyes had shifted, looked over his shoulder and chuckled. "Yes, she is quite a looker, isn't she? That's Ginger Brooks. Got a mind to go with the face and figure, too. Graduated from Yale Law School. But don't get any ideas … she married her college sweetheart and, after working for a while, had two daughters and decided to stay home and be a mom."

Chris gave Henry a wink. "So, anything about her that can help me in my time of need, Henry, now that my heart is broken?"

"Indeed there is, she's quite a Brute," Henry replied.

"Seriously, no woman who looks like that can be called a brute!" Chris whispered.

Henry's response, also quiet, was immediate and forceful. "It has nothing to do with appearance, or smarts, for that matter. She's a Brute because she has a Vision of what she wants to do with her life now that her girls are in high school and college. She's always making a list of things she has to accomplish, and crossing those things off. She works hard. So, she's getting things done, but they're not really helping her make any progress towards her ultimate Vision. And she has no Process in place to make that Vision a reality. She's essentially stuck in place—a victim of the Peter Principal. She has Output, and some Vision but no Process other than brute force. That's what I call a Brute."

"Then Brutes are bad news?" Chris asked.

"No, none of these characters are 'bad' in and of themselves. But all of them, other than the Success, are limited in what they can do for you. Brutes can be absolute heroes in the short term. Lots of startups get by for a while on the brute force of the founders. Brutes can bail you out of some really bad situations. But long term, Brutes get tired. They don't scale. Eventually their Output fades. And if you start to count on them to bail you out, they may fail at the worst possible time."

They left the coffee shop and walked past the post office to city hall. Henry led Chris into the office section on the main floor. Since it was a weekend, most of the offices were dark. But through a glass door Chris could see a short, squat man sitting at a very large desk. The stenciled letters on the door read, "Building Permits." The man's head was buried in a tall pile of papers.

Henry said, "There's Burt Johnson, our local building inspector. He's very dedicated, a good public servant putting in the overtime the city can't afford to reimburse him for. He's got no Vision, and his Output seems to be measured in geologic time, but boy, does he have Process! Fill out the forms in triplicate … make sure you do things in this exact order … go back and do it again. He drives the local builders crazy. He is, in every sense of the word, our fourth character: a Bureaucrat."

Chris was quick to pile on. "Someone once told me that 'Love may make the world go round, but only a bureaucrat can slow the world down!'"

"So," Henry said, "you've got no use for Bureaucrats, then?"

"None! They impede progress, get in the way of good decisions, and are pains in the butt."

"Before you walk into that room Monday morning, you might want to reconsider your position. Sure, Bureaucrats can be frustrating. But they also can be essential."

"What? You must be joking."

Henry steered Chris through the front door and out of earshot of Burt. "What do you think would happen if we didn't have a building inspector in this town? Think maybe some less than upstanding contractors might cut a few corners to save some money or some time? Oops, your new house foundation just cracked, sorry! On your flight to New York tonight, do you care if the pilot has had his FAA proficiency checked lately? Do you have a QA organization in your current company, or do you just let the manufacturing folks turn out products without anyone checking to be sure they meet spec?"

"Easy, Henry, don't go high and mighty on me. Of course some checks and balances are helpful. It's just that once you give bureaucrats power, it seems to go to their heads!"

"Right, it can," Henry agreed. Once Bureaucrats see

their Processes as ends in themselves, you are in trouble. But here's where The Success Matrix can help you. If you can get a Bureaucrat to understand the Vision of the greater organization, the 'greater good,' if you will, and help connect them to those responsible for Output, they become solutions rather than problems. The key is to turn the Bureaucrats into serving you, rather than you serving them.

"There's a builder here named Charlie Rodriguez who figured out that the other builders usually fill out their work orders for the week on Monday, and so they all arrive on Tuesday morning, clamoring to get Burt to accept their paperwork and schedule inspections for later in the week. So Charlie takes a different approach. He gets all his papers in Friday afternoon. He noticed Burt often comes in on weekends to catch up. The papers you saw on Burt's desk were probably mostly from Charlie. Come Monday morning, Charlie will have his applications approved, and even have his inspections scheduled for the week, while the other builders are standing in line. Charlie has developed a reputation in town for being on time and on budget ... more than most contractors. He figured out how to make Burt's life easier by balancing his workload. Charlie has turned Burt's role to his advantage. Without even knowing it, the Bureaucrat has become a weapon (a Process!) in Charlie's competitive arsenal. And for whatever reason, the other builders have never discovered his secret.

"Now, that said, you don't want too many Bureaucrats in your organization. But my advice is, when you find one you know you need, don't burn 'em, turn 'em!"

———————————————

It was time for lunch, and Henry suggested they grab a sandwich at the corner deli and sit outside to enjoy the sunshine. They found a bench on the sidewalk and once again the conversation turned to their personal lives. Chris finally asked Henry to get back on point. The day was half over, and he still had four more characters to hear about, and then had to try to figure out whether or not this had been a giant waste of time.

"I'm ready for the next character," Chris said.

"Fine." Henry wiped a stray bit of mayonnaise off his upper lip. "Follow me." They proceeded down Front Street to Kelly's General Store. Patrick Kelly greeted Henry with a wave from behind the cash register. "What'll it be today, Henry?" he called out.

"Just snooping, Patrick," Henry replied cheerfully. He always enjoyed wandering the aisles at Kelly's. It was an old-fashioned general store, with everything from hardware to fishing tackle to kitchen appliances to trail mix to snowmobile boots.

He turned to Chris. "Patrick is the second generation Kelly to run this place. He took over from his dad a few years ago. This place is an institution in Newport. If you need it, Kelly's has it. If Kelly's doesn't have it, then you must not really need it."

Chris laughed. "Sounds like everyone must love this place." He focused in on some very unusual fishing lures on the wall. "I've never seen lures like these."

"How do you think that beautiful lake trout came to spend eternity over my fireplace?" Henry asked. "Kelly senior invented those lures years ago, and the fish haven't yet figured them out. Of course, now you can get knock-offs

at Walmart in Burlington, or at Canadian Tire in Sher-
brooke. Speaking of those big box stores, I suppose you'd
like to know which character our friend Patrick is." Chris
raised his eyebrows in anticipation.

"He's a Merchant," Henry said.

"Gosh, I never would have thought of that!" Chris let
the sarcasm show in his voice.

Henry did his best Kung Fu imitation. "Ah, young
grasshopper, once again you confuse the generic word with
the character."

Chris played along. "Please, Master, enlighten me."

"A Merchant lacks Vision, but, like Patrick, has excellent Process and Output. Since he is successful, he believes
he can just keep doing what he's been doing, and all will be
well with the world."

"What's wrong with that? If it ain't broke, don't fix it!"
Chris was puzzled.

"Fair enough," Henry replied. "But that only works in
a relatively static business situation. Kelly's lives in a shel-
tered competitive environment. So far, Walmart hasn't
seen fit to open a store in Newport. But what happens if
they do? Some of us old-timers still would shop at Kelly's
out of loyalty. But over time, people will be drawn to the
selection and prices at the big box store. Bye bye, Kelly's."

"Remember when I told you that Brutes don't scale?
The problem with Merchants is that they don't adapt. They
can do just fine for years, and then suddenly, poof, they're
gone. If you want evidence, look right across the street. See
that storefront with the 'For Lease' sign on it? That used
to be a bookstore. Then some company named Amazon
came along and that long-time successful Merchant went

belly-up!"

"So if I find a Merchant in my new organization, what do I do?" Chris was finally getting to the point where he wanted to get past the "what" to the "so what" and "then what" stages of his education.

"It depends on the context," Henry replied. "If that part of the business is in a stable technology, you may be fine for some time. If not, you better pair that Merchant either with a Dreamer or an Academic, or be prepared to see bad things happen very quickly!"

The light was slowly going on in Chris' head.

"Better yet, replace the Merchant with a Success!" Henry couldn't help himself.

"But I don't yet know what a Success looks like in your damn Matrix!"

"Patience, grasshopper."

They crossed the street, walked past the bankrupt bookstore and stopped in front of Millie's diner again.

"I missed an opportunity this morning to point out one of the other characters you need to know," Henry admitted. "See the guy who served us our oatmeal? That's Philippe. Not sure what his last name is. He's been waiting tables at Millie's for a couple of years. Works hard, cheerful, efficient. But I've always felt he could do more than move dishes around."

"Hey," Chris interjected, "Nothing wrong with being a waiter. You know I did that in college."

"Of course there's nothing wrong with it. Our society

couldn't function without Grunts."

"Grunt?" Chris asked. "That's pretty harsh."

"A 'Grunt', my friend, is character number six. No Vision, no Process, but Output. Grunts are limited to their own energy level. They are essentially running in place: punching the clock and doing their assigned tasks without any prospect for advancement or improvement. All their goals are short term. Many small shopkeepers are Grunts, and I'm not saying that to be mean. Grunts are the lubricant in our society and in our business lives. We absolutely need them. And they appear just fine as long as their Output is still important to those around them. But if something changes, you'll find them collecting unemployment."

"Grunts are always low level workers, then?" Chris thought this was an easy one.

"Surprisingly, no," said Henry. "Think about turn-around executives. Most are not Grunts, but some definitely are. They come in, fire people, cut costs, and collect their big bonus checks. That may look like a success to some, but it's all short term thinking. At that point, they depart, leaving the company they supposedly 'fixed' with no Vision and no Process, but plenty of positive Output. But ever notice how often, after those guys move on, those 'turned around' companies turn belly up instead?

"Here's another example. Know anyone in your career who seemed to have 'retired in place'? They had no Vision and no Process, but they got by on their Output and their reputation from before they nodded off at their desk. Those people can survive a long time in a static organization. But if anything upsets the status quo, like new management, new competitors, or new expectations, they often are the first to fail."

"Understood." Chris was growing more confident with the concepts. "Grunts are good, unless they're bad."

"Ah, the young grasshopper becomes a wise ass!"

They walked back to the center of town. Chris noticed a young man slouching against the wall of a building, strumming on an old guitar—and not very well at that. He had a vacant look on his face, a sort of "lost in space" appearance.

Chris turned to Henry. "Boy, that guy looks like a loser."

"Well done!" Henry replied.

"What do you mean, well done?" Chris was confused.

"The Loser is our seventh character. No Vision, no Process, no Output. As they said on the old TV show, 'You are the weakest link. Goodbye!'"

"Right," said Chris. "That makes sense. But I don't imagine there's much to learn from him. Certainly in my new assignment, there won't be any Losers in the room."

"Don't be so sure," Henry warned. "Organizations and people can drift into the Loser category without even knowing it. Take a high performing group that loses sight of its Vision, and you have a Merchant. Take a Merchant that loses touch with its Processes, and you have a Grunt. Take a Grunt and inject new Output requirements, and you can come face to face with a Loser.

"It's like the frog and the pot of water. Put a frog in a pot of boiling water, and he'll jump out and live to hop another day. But put him in a pot of warm water and turn the heat up slowly, and he'll, um, *croak* before he knows what happened. For organizations it's the same. Give them a sudden shock and they might snap out of their drift into irrelevance. But let them decline slowly, and they may not wake up in time to survive."

"I'll remember that," said Chris.

Across the town square, in the direction of the road to Henry's house, they passed a church. On the grass were about twenty children sitting in a semicircle around a middle-aged blonde woman reading aloud from a book. She looked vaguely familiar, but Chris couldn't place the face. However, he did notice the kids were remarkably well behaved, particularly outside on a warm spring day.

"Who's that?" Chris asked.

"Oh, glad you noticed her," said Henry. "That's Ms. Rhodes, the first grade teacher over at Newport Elementary. And in fact, in my Success Matrix, she's the embodiment of a Success."

Chris didn't really understand. "Sure, she's teaching kids, and that's a noble profession. I imagine she's terrific at her job. But how does that relate to the real, tough world of business?"

Henry frowned. "Don't you recognize her?"

"How would I recognize someone in this out-of-the-way place that I've never visited before?" Chris asked.

Henry put his hand on Chris's arm. "Perhaps if I used her maiden name, Street, it would help?"

Chris was sure Henry was taking his turn enjoying

a painful play on words. "You mean this woman named Street married a guy named Rhodes? You are pulling my leg, aren't you?"

"No, her last name was Street, and now her students all know her as Ms. Rhodes. But, you may recognize her by her first name, Picabo."

"Picabo Street? The Olympic gold medalist in skiing? That's why she looked familiar!"

"Yes, indeed," said Henry. "And not only did she win skiing medals around the world, she did so after blowing out her knee. That woman is a great example of someone who had a burning Vision, initially had a Process to achieve her goals when healthy, then a tougher Process when she had to rehab her knee, and still ended up with the Output of being the best in the world. Perhaps just as impressive, once she hung up her skis, she went back to school, got her teaching certificate, and, as you can see, has those seven-year-olds completely mesmerized. For those kids to be out there with her today, she must also be volunteering for Sunday school class at the church."

"What's she doing here? I thought she was from Sun Valley."

"Ah, the power of love," Henry answered. "When she competed down the road at Stowe she met a guy named Rhodes on the Canadian ski team who's from right over the border in Georgeville, Quebec. They decided northern Vermont was a good compromise for a place to live."

"So that's all eight characters, right? Chris asked. "Dreamer, Academic, Brute, Bureaucrat, Merchant, Grunt, Loser and Success."

"Good boy." Henry smiled. "You have been paying attention after all."

As they walked back to Henry's, they passed a yard where a young man of high school age was mowing the grass. Henry decided it was time to see if his young charge had learned The Success Matrix beyond just the eight names.

"That kid behind the mower over there: What character do you think he is?"

Chris could see there was some Output and so he was pretty sure the young man was probably a Grunt, although possibly a Merchant or a Brute. But since the task was menial, he decided to go with the obvious. "He's a Grunt, I imagine."

"Wrong," replied Henry. "He's a Success, too!"

"You are kidding, right?" asked Chris.

Henry stopped walking and looked hard at Chris.

"You ALWAYS have to understand the context! All you're seeing is a kid cutting grass. What you don't know is that this isn't his house or yard. That kid, his name is MJ by the way, has this town in the palm of his hand. His parents are nice, but poor. So MJ took it upon himself to make and save enough money for college. Most kids won't do the manual labor stuff these days. They'd rather be home playing video games and texting their friends. Not MJ.

"He must cut the grass for five or ten families in town. In September, he rakes leaves. Every year in late October he shows up at front doors with his snow shovel offering to be first on the scene to shovel walks once the snow flies. He gets all the older women to sign up, and some of the men, too. In the spring, he sells flower and vegetable seeds. That kid has a Vision of going to college, the Process in place to earn the money, and the hard work and Output to make it happen.

"Like any good Success, he also was smart about enlisting the help of others where his own Process wasn't going to be enough. Turns out the kid isn't a bad hockey player. Not a superstar, mind you, but the kind of grinder who wins face-offs and digs the puck out of the corners. He'd love to get a scholarship to the University of Vermont, but he needed some video clips of himself to send to the coach in Burlington. So he offered Scott Anderson, our town Dreamer, a trade. You found out earlier that Scott's hobby is photography. MJ offered to shovel his walk for free all winter if Scott would come to some games and shoot video of him playing, and then edit the footage into a highlight DVD. Scott had so much fun doing that, and was so impressed with the kid's work ethic, that he ended up giving him a "tip" for the same amount he would have paid for snow shoveling in the first place. Successes have a way of getting more out of the people around them than you can predict.

"As I told you while your brain went numb at the sight of Ginger Brooks, looks can be very deceiving. Oh, I should add that MJ over there seems to have caught the eye of one of her lovely daughters. I'd say the kid is a Success on a number of fronts. You'll find that people who are a Success in one area often are in others areas, too."

As they approached the house, Chris decided to turn the tables on his host. "How would you describe yourself at your newfound passion for painting?"

Henry laughed. "Good question. I think I probably rank as a Brute right now. I know what I want to be able to do, and I do turn out some reasonable art, although nothing very impressive. But my skills, my Process, still need a lot of work." Then a smile spread across his face. "To be fair, I am working on the Process part. There's an evening painting course at the community college. I am making slow, steady progress, with the help of my instructor."

He paused. "My instructor just happens to be the same Ginger Brooks who turned your head at the coffee shop. She is a woman of many talents!"

"You sly dog, you!" Chris said.

"Perhaps," said Henry wistfully, "As an artist, I'm a Brute. But as a romantic, I'm more of a Dreamer. Plenty of Vision, little Process, no Output. Then again, maybe her husband won't live forever."

They walked up the gravel driveway. The shadows were lengthening. If Chris was going to make his evening flight to New York it was time to go.

Henry had thought about his parting words carefully. "So, Mr. Hot Shot. Do you think you've got it now? Just remember, each individual on your staff doesn't have to have all three attributes, although the more they have the better. But as a team, working as a unit, you must have all three—and in balance. The Success Matrix is pretty easy to understand, even if you have to look past the surface sometimes to get it in the right context. Think you can pull it off with a bunch of anxious potential direct reports with people staring at you through a one-way mirror?"

Chris paused a long time. "We'll know tomorrow, won't we?"

TWO

The Success Matrix Defined

As Chris boarded his flight to New York, he was doing his best to think of an approach that would allow him to use his newfound tools during his crucial meeting the next day. Settling into his seat, one thing was clear to him. He needed to get everyone in the room engaged and interacting, not just listening to him talk. Getting his potential direct reports talking would allow him to observe and perhaps start to categorize them into their character roles. So he sent an email to his host, asking for flip charts and markers as well as a computer projection system, shut down his iPhone and closed his eyes, suddenly feeling drained from the last 48 hours. Before the plane started its takeoff, he had drifted off to sleep.

We'll check back in with Chris again in chapter eleven (no peeking ahead!), but for now let's move from fiction to fact and put meat on the bones of The Success Matrix model, with actual examples from real business situations. There's no better place to start than with some more comprehensive definitions.

VISION

*"A broadly understood sense of direction
which encompasses competitive leadership
over time."*

Let's look more closely at the key phrases to make sure the important concepts are fully explained. First, for a Vision to be useful to an organization, it needs to be "broadly understood."

If the Vision relates just to upper management, then you absolutely will not get goal congruence across the organization, and being widely disseminated or communicated is *not* the same as being broadly understood. Lots of corporate Vision statements find their way onto posters in the lunchroom. But only rarely do they become part of the company's culture. When they do, it is powerful.

A personal example of this occurred when someone who had just flown into town mentioned seeing one of my company's factory floor employees at the airport. They struck up a conversation, during which that employee described our company's Vision in crisp detail. It was broadly understood, indeed! And the power that came from that understanding meant the entire organization knew where we were going, and why, and so decisions were made that were in concert with that Vision.

However, for those who have read my Harvard Business Review article, *The Vision Trap*, you may remember that "broadly understood" can be counterproductive if the Vision itself leads you astray. The fundamental take-away from that article was, "beware of vision creep." It is just as insidious as "feature creep" in product development. In fact, as *The Vision Trap* notes, vision creep can *drive* feature creep. Keep your Vision sensible, focused and well-grounded, or pay a terrible price.

Next in our definition of Vision is "sense of direction." This is different than any specific task, product plans or targets. It means precisely what it says. If you are headed in a direction, you know roughly where you are going, even if you don't know exactly where you'll end up. The US settlers knew they were moving west, even if they didn't know how far they would go, or what awaited them when they got there. If they kept moving toward the setting sun, they were headed in the right direction.

For those readers who are pilots, this reminds me of an article called *Inertial Navigation Simplified*. It stated, in summary, "The aircraft knows where it is at all times. It knows this because it knows where it isn't. And it doesn't know where it's going, but it knows where it's been."

Actually, there is more than a little truth to the above muddle when it comes to "sense of direction" in The Success Matrix definition of Vision. You certainly know where you were as an organization, and have a very good notion as to where you are. That sets your context. You also know where you don't want to go, or have no ability to go. That sets your boundaries. Your sense of direction, then, begins with where you were and are, eliminating where you will not go, and projecting yourself into a future of changing customer requirements and competitive challenge. In a moment, you'll see how one company's Vision set up a "broadly understood sense of direction" that has carried it successfully for more than 30 years.

That brings us to "competitive leadership over time."

The key here is to understand that competitive leadership means the ability to do two things. First, you need to be able to go toe-to-toe with your competitors and prevail. Second, however, you also need to find ways *not* to go toe-to-toe every day in every way. If you do, a competitor may land a punch and knock you out. Competitive leadership requires a deep understanding of customer "care-abouts," so you can emphasize (and fight for) just the issues that matter, and take a pass on the issues that don't. Competitive leadership is a blend of product and price that speaks to the customer's perceived value. It also requires a sophisticated appreciation for the value of differentiation. That's where the "not toe-to-toe" issue plays out.

Apple is a powerful, positive example of a successful Vision. However, if you go back to the time they lost their way, you'll find their one big flaw was revealed as the computer industry standardized on "Wintel" (Microsoft Windows + Intel) software. Apple still had product differentiation, but it was not price competitive and did not offer the same breadth of software. That dramatically constrained how and where they could win. Compare that to Apple's later rebound years, and you'll see they stressed product differentiation, broad software AND reasonably competitive prices. They learned!

It's useful to look more closely at Apple as one of the finest examples of a sustained corporate Vision. To be clear, what follows is not an official, explicit "Apple Vision." But it certainly embodies what Steve Jobs and his team embedded in the soul of that enterprise.

*"Provide unmatched user access to computing power
and digital content"*

Initially, in the 1980s, this meant desktop computers with a very friendly user interface, plus software (desktop publishing) that made creating digital content possible for the masses. Later, the content was expanded to include multimedia: graphics and video, but still with a focus on creation rather than consumption. That was successful. But for a variety of reasons, including some strategic and tactical mistakes (like pricing), and some senior management selection blunders during Jobs' absence, it relegated the company to a nice but small niche in the computer industry.

Then Jobs returned and took exactly the same Vision but extended its meaning to the next wave of customer requirements and technological possibilities. In so doing, he leapfrogged his competition. First came the iPod, and we saw accessibility of digital content move from creation to consumption: a much bigger play. In parallel came iTunes for much broader content availability. Then Apple announced the iPhone for much broader access to computing power (now mobile), again with a new, unmatched standard of user friendliness. In rapid succession came the App Store, iBooks and the iPad for more power, more friendly accessibility and more digital content.

It all fits comfortably within the same Vision—now extended for well over 30 years. And it is broadly understood, not just by Apple employees but also by their customers—a key to brand building. Apple means superior ease of use. Apple means powerful creation tools. Apple means the most digital and multimedia content. As one of their ads declared, "If you don't have an iPhone, you don't have an iPhone." They could use circular logic because "Provide unmatched user access to computing power and digital content" is indeed *"A broadly understood sense of direction which encompasses competitive leadership over time."*

Perhaps a less profound example of a successful Vision was that of Frank Perdue, the frozen chicken king. He fed his chickens marigold petals, which gave them a golden skin color. In the supermarket, they stood out next to the pasty white competition (differentiation). Then he ran ads saying, over and over, that a golden chicken is a more tender chicken. He was able to charge a bit more (perceived value) in what was otherwise a pure commodity space. And that approach lasted for decades ("over time").

PROCESS

"The structures, methods and procedures to repeatedly produce timely, high quality products or services, independent of changes in personnel."

Again, let's examine the definition and its components. "Structures, methods and procedures" is straightforward. This is the cookbook, the checklist, the documented roadmap. What is not always straightforward is to know *whether the cookbook actually exists.* In many organizations, there are common practices that become embedded in the environment without ever being evaluated, much less documented. One of the reasons for the rise in workflow automation software across essentially every major industry is the desire by executive management to capture those best practices and then get everyone to commit to them. But one of the reasons we've seen so many workflow automation projects fail, or take much longer than expected to succeed, is that people have made their own tweaks to approved corporate mandates that don't fit comfortably into these programs.

As a venture capital investor, I've seen firsthand the issue of "repeatedly produce" in our material science deals. Getting these projects from the lab to pilot production to full scale manufacturing is not just a scale-up exercise. It is also an exercise in consistency. Concocting a recipe that can stand up to the inevitable variances in raw material and process tolerances is tough. But the same holds true in service businesses, where the variable is human nature itself.

Next, "timely, high quality products or services." This starts to bring the Vision issues down to earth. *In the end, nothing matters unless someone buys something.* And no one buys something unless it is available when and where they want it, and it meets their need. It is possible to have good procedures in place (structures and methods), and possible to make what you want over and over (repeatedly produce), but if you miss the market window, or fall short of the quality customers require, then all the procedures and production amount to very little.

Finally, in the Process definition we come to the phrase that can trip up so many organizations: "independent of changes in personnel." We all know heroes in the work place. They produce at rates far above their peers. They bail us out of tight spots in business and on the battlefield. They answer the alarm on organizational fire drills. They put in those 100 hour weeks to meet seemingly impossible deadlines. But the problem with heroes is that they don't scale. No matter how heroic, they are people, not a sustainable structure, method or procedure. Ultimately, they get tired, or they get burned out, or they get hired away to work on the next great thing. The reason major enterprises spend so much energy on human development and succession planning is that they understand how dependent they can become on heroes. And the reason startups do exactly the opposite is that they realize how powerful heroes can be, as long as they last.

In chapter five (The Brute), we'll talk about this dichotomy and how to manage around it.

OUTPUT

"Profitable products and services are being produced with predictable regularity."

This is the easiest of the three definitions to explain. We all get measured on Output. It drives our annual performance review and our bonuses. And therein lies the potential for a big problem. But first, two words in the definition warrant attention. "Profitable" products and services is a key driver. It tells us whether our costs are in line, and our value is recognized in the marketplace. Any Output short of profitable smacks of wasted effort. "Predictable" regularity speaks to whether the Output is both sustained and sustainable. Short bursts of excellence are not enough.

So where does the big problem arise? Output is a lagging indicator. Output also is seductive. If Output is good, why change anything (as Chris said, "If it ain't broke, don't fix it")? If you are getting a big bonus, you certainly don't want to change that!

A more valuable perspective would be, "If it ain't broke, it soon will be. Get on it!" How many times have we seen organizations rise and, just as they are declared victorious, start to decline? It happens in business, in sports and all around us. The passion (Vision) to get to the top and the hard work and focus on fundamentals (Process) all get forgotten once the winner's spoils (Output) are in our grasp. The "dynasty" companies and athletic teams rarely deliver on their promise of long term competitive leadership. After they reach their desired Output, their Vision starts to fade, then their Processes erode, and by the time Output falls, the organization is in serious decline.

One of my favorite sayings is, "The leading indicator of failure is success." Perhaps the reverse also is true; we'll talk about that in chapter nine (The Loser). But for the moment, let's take a hard look at why Output is both vital and viral. It is what we all strive to achieve, but often we become ill from having achieved it. In fact, this was the "Aha!" revelation that led me to develop The Success Matrix in the first place. It was not until my company, Mentor Graphics, had achieved greatness and then had been humbled that the light went on in my head and I understood what had happened.

Mentor was the fifth most profitable company started in the US in the 1980s (Source: Inc. Magazine) and remains the fastest public software company ever to reach $200M in constant dollar sales (Source: Tableau Software). Heady stuff! Yet, in the early 1990s, Mentor almost went bankrupt, burning over $100M in cash in just two years as it struggled with Output. The foundation for the decline, however, was laid in the success of the late 1980s, as Mentor was racking up record profits and accumulating the cash that allowed it later to survive. Once the company thought the world was our oyster, we lost our Vision, then lost our Processes, and by the time we hit the wall on Output it was almost too late to recover.

The message is: when Output is going well, it is no time to relax. In fact, it is perhaps the most dangerous time. That is when management needs to be on high alert to make sure the Vision and the Process are being well cared for.

That brings us to The Success Matrix—the presence (X) or absence (–) of the three variables—and the characters that align in each case.

The Success Matrix

	Vision	Process	Output
The Dreamer	X	–	–
The Academic	X	X	–
The Brute	X	–	X
The Bureaucrat	–	X	–
The Merchant	–	X	X
The Grunt	–	–	X
The Loser	–	–	–
The Success	X	X	X

The chapters that follow will explore each of these characters in more detail and help you identify each one. Then you'll know what to expect from them, how to deal with them, and how to assemble them into a team that functions as a Success even when the individuals or organizations do not.

YOUR PERSONAL SUCCESS MATRIX

As you read in the story in chapter one, The Success Matrix is not just a business tool; it is a personal tool as well. However, to use it in your life outside work, a few modifications to the definitions are in order. Here they are:

VISION

"A deeply-held conviction as to where you want your life to go over time."

PROCESS

"The means, methods and techniques to achieve your goals and vision, independent of temporary setbacks or distractions."

OUTPUT

"Tangible evidence that you are achieving progress towards your life goals."

At the end of each "character" chapter that follows, you will find a page designed to help you connect the business application of The Success Matrix to your personal life.

THREE

The Dreamer

"Imagination will often carry us to worlds that never were. But without it we go nowhere."

Carl Sagan

Carl Sagan was a visionary, and a Dreamer as well. His view of the universe opened our minds to its endless possibilities. But he also didn't have any real approach to help mankind reach out beyond our own modest location in the universe.

Is this a bad thing? Not at all.

Somewhere a child is looking at the stars, dreaming about someday flying to Mars, or beyond. The Carl Sagans of the world might inspire that child and others to carry out what Sagan only mused about. But Dreamers themselves don't get very far on Vision alone.

In the venture capital business, a steady parade of Dreamers comes through our doors. The conversation usually goes something like this:

"I have this big idea that will change the world and make you a zillion dollars if you invest in my company. However, I can't tell you what it is unless you sign a non-disclosure agreement. Once we get this business up to scale, all the customers in our market will flock to us and one of the big guys will have to buy us out, or we'll go public like (insert name of most recent big IPO winner)."

"No, I haven't ever run a company before."

"No, I don't have a team assembled yet. "

"No, I can't describe the exact steps we will have to take to get up to scale. "

"No, I haven't talked with any potential customers yet because I don't want the idea getting out there …"

The message we give to the entrepreneur is that big Visions and big ideas are a dime a dozen. If you think you are the only person in the world who has had your particular idea, you are very likely kidding yourself. It is the ability to *execute* on big ideas that separates big winners from big losers.

Without practical balance, Vision achieves nothing.

On the other hand, without the passion that comes from a big Vision (a Big Hairy Audacious Goal, or BHAG, in Jim Collins' *Built to Last* parlance) you aren't going to create a large enough or disruptive enough force to unseat incumbent competitors or leapfrog potential competitors.

The challenge, then, is to capture that grand Vision and keep the visionary fully engaged, while trying to layer in pragmatic people and Processes to make the Vision a reality. Sound hard to do? It's even *harder* than it sounds. Dreamers tend to be remarkably stubborn people. In many ways, they have to be. Anyone trying to upset the status quo faces a chorus of naysayers:

"That will never work."

"We tried that before and it didn't work."

"No one else has ever done it that way, so it must not work."

"If we try that, big company X will copy us a year later and we'll be out of work."

"Why don't you focus on the problems we have today and get back to work?"

Dreamers dismiss all those slings and arrows (and others even more personal) with the rock-ribbed (not to mention hard-headed) belief that they really have figured out something that will change the world. And in that passion lies the wellspring of all the successful startups we have ever seen.

The flip side is that, while Dreamers don't suffer fools gladly, they also believe anyone who presents evidence counter to their Vision is a fool. Facts (often) don't matter. Yet, as John Adams famously said, "Facts are stubborn things."

In my venture capital experience, we've seen this movie more times than I can count. You start with a technical/scientific/engineering founder who has a searing Vision for some new product or service that will upend their industry, or create an entirely new one. They gather a few other true believers around them to start a company. Because the founder is the founder, he or she assumes they should be the CEO, regardless of their prior background or management experience in functional areas beyond technology.

At some point, the product development process bogs down, indicating that the initial Vision was either slightly or fundamentally flawed. But the founder refuses to allow the same bright people (that he enlisted in the first place) to be heard and alternatives considered. And millions of dollars go down the drain chasing a Vision that proves to be ephemeral.

Doing even more damage is the Dreamer who cannot stay focused on executing the Vision before coming up with another, equally interesting Vision that jerks the organization in another direction. Rather than having a dreamcatcher (those with elementary school age children have probably made one), what is really needed is a dream filter. But Dreamers in a position of power usually will not tolerate filters.

Our venture firm has backed all sorts of Dreamers. One in the biotech world became bitter at being pushed aside when "stubborn" facts forced a change in scientific direction from his initial Vision. He proceeded to do everything he could to undermine the company, sending scathing letters to employees and investors alike, even though he still had substantial equity. He was far more interested in being right than in getting rich. Ironically, the firm in question, with new leadership and an engineering team now free to pursue a viable path, was ultimately successful, going public in 2013 and making that dysfunctional founder a lot of money.

Another Dreamer/founder we backed (this one in the wireless market) suffered from "Vision-du-jour" syndrome. While some of his Visions were spot on, the organization was pulled in multiple directions, depending on what was new on any given day in his fertile mind. Again, a change in leadership allowed for focus on a couple of the most promising areas, and with solid execution the company quickly thrived. That founder was smart enough, once the initial blow to his ego had healed, to support the new team when he saw they were making his stock worth a lot of money.

The underlying message here is simple: You definitely want Dreamers on the team. You just don't want them *in charge* of the team. At least, not if you expect the team to produce anything other than more dreams.

When some of the technological giants in US industry had true research labs (Bell Labs, IBM, HP) they could afford to put all their Dreamers in one organization and let them invent. But those inventions only went so far towards commercialization within those dedicated labs. At some point, the operating divisions had to take the ideas, or not, and deliver them to market. Those firms had a built-in filter mechanism.

Most companies don't have the luxury of a dedicated think tank where Dreamers can be isolated, nurtured and allowed to graze freely. Most of us have to find a way to attract, retain and utilize those visionaries within the context of our operating units. But first, you have to identify them.

THREE EASY STEPS TO IDENTIFY A DREAMER

It is always essential to identify which character you are dealing with. In this case, how do you know you have a Dreamer in your organization?

- Fancy talk, but no action. There is no tangible evidence of achievement or progress towards realizing the Vision. Dreamers are often masters of the latest buzz words, which they can string together in a way that makes them seem inordinately smart and well-informed. But, just as often, that's all there is: fancy language without a real understanding of what the words mean, and why they should matter. If you start to get the feeling that you are being given more style than substance, you may have found a Dreamer (or an Academic—more in chapter four).

- Lots of focus on "what," but little on "how" or "when." Dreamers have an extraordinary ability to believe that, simply by saying what they want to do, it can be done. But "wishing doesn't make it so." When you suspect you are being "dreamed-at," start asking questions: "How do you think we can make that happen? What obstacles do you think we'll encounter? How will we get past those hurdles? Who in our organization do you think will need to be involved? How long do you think it will take?" An absence of thoughtful answers to those questions is a key indicator that you've met a Dreamer.

- Single-minded approach to problems: "My way is the only way this can be done." Many Dreamers get very narrow-minded once they develop their ideas. That biotech founder

I mentioned earlier was a prime example. What was unfortunate was that his Vision was actually sound, but his unwillingness even to consider alternative implementation techniques doomed him. When you get a bright, inventive person who suddenly seems to have blinders on, you're likely talking to a Dreamer.

YOU'VE FOUND A DREAMER, NOW WHAT?

A Dreamer is an incredibly powerful asset, if harnessed (yes, "harnessed" is the right word) properly. Of all the characters in this book, Dreamers are by far the rarest beasts in the business jungle. But they also can be remarkably disruptive, wasteful and, frankly, annoying. They have a remarkably good time generating ideas while the rest of us soldier on with the reality of earning a living. So, how do you harness this beast?

- Make them proud of their status. The reason many highly successful companies have created titles such as "Technical Fellow" or "Chief Innovator" or the like is to reward Dreamers with designations that recognize their skills, yet also ensure they are not put in charge of organizations that require steady Processes or regular Output to make the enterprise successful. This is not to say that all Dreamers are found in R&D. I am always puzzled why, in advertising agencies, certain folks are labeled as being from the "creative" department, as if the rest of the organization is from "not-so-creative" departments. But it is useful, because it identifies those who are allowed to dream up ad campaigns with impunity, while others stand ready to take the ideas and push the better ones forward (and filter out the bad ones).

- Find them friends. In chapter one, you'll recall that Scott Anderson, the former architect and now resident Dreamer in Newport, had been successful when surrounded by others in his architectural firm who could take his ideas and create useful designs that actually could be built. But, upon his own in retirement, he floundered because he had no "friends" to pick up where he left off. Of course, Dreamers need friends to whom they can pass off the Process and Output responsibilities, and they have to trust those people won't ruin their brainchildren. They need friends because, in their zeal to promote and defend their ideas, they sometimes can offend people. Having a few well-placed folks to smooth ruffled feathers can keep the ideas flowing.

- Show them the commercial value of their ideas. Nothing excites Dreamers more than seeing their ideas actually come to life as a successful product. Get them in front of industry gatherings and company meetings where the ultimate value of their inventions is recognized. It might just help them develop their own internal filter as well.

YOUR PERSONAL DREAMER

Are you a Dreamer in your personal life? Do you fantasize about the life you'd like to live, the things you'd like to accomplish, if only you had the time, or the money, or the connections? Can you describe any realistic steps you have taken to achieve any of those Visions?

Dreamers need Process to get to Output.

- Start to focus on the "how" and the "when" in your life. It's amazing what you can do just by taking simple steps in that direction. Here's a personal reflection. This book has been over 20 years in the making, since I first formulated the concept and named the characters as part of a corporate offsite event I was leading. That generated the dream of the book, but I had no Process other than gazing longingly at the PowerPoint slides from that meeting, and once in a while updating it for a new audience. Finally, I reached out to a business friend who also is a successful author. He saw what I had and immediately challenged me to add the fictional bookend concept (chapters one and eleven) and asked when I might have that for his review. He changed my "how" by saying "have some fun with this, get creative" and drove the "when" by asking for a deadline. As a wise VP of R&D I knew well once said, "Deadlines work wonders."

- Now, track your progress. Make a simple Success Matrix of your own. Write down those Visions, ideas and goals in the left column. Now force yourself to write down Processes for each and indicate how you'll know (i.e., what to look for) you are achieving the Output you want. After each Output, set a date when you think you can accomplish those things. Make yourself review your Matrix regularly (you decide the proper frequency). Better yet, share it with someone you care about and who cares about you. Cheerleaders are great motivators (and taskmasters)!

FOUR

The Academic

"Academic politics are the most vicious, because so little is at stake."

Wallace Sayre

A cademics in your organization are like consultants, only less expensive. Correction: they can be VERY expensive. These characters eat cash at an astounding rate. They can be very articulate in describing what should be done. They can be very specific about how the goals should be achieved. But then they step aside with a smile and generously let you provide the details and elbow grease. It can be easy to spot a person or an organization that lives in the Academic mode. They often have big goals and big systems in place to handle their business, but do not have any evidence of big profits. The organization can take the tone of religious revival meetings as long as there is ample cash to fund the academic exercise. Academics can be fun (remember those late night bull sessions in college?) until it comes time to pay the bills (Mom and

Dad, please send money!).

Academic organizations also can also become very politically charged, per Wallace Sayre's quote above. Because they can take on the tone of religious revivals, anyone who questions that religion can be quickly labeled a heretic and burned at the stake (usually figuratively, it is to be hoped).

There are almost certainly people and organizations in your world who behave as consultants. Perhaps they are even encouraged to. We can all benefit from people who can step back from the forest, see the trees, and then tell us which trees need to be cut down to allow us to get to the other side of that forest. I had the good fortune both to work one summer at one of the big brand consulting organizations, and later on a corporate team when another of those consulting firms was brought in. Overall, I think the quality of their work is terrific. But don't ever expect to pay them based on the "Output of their Output." They may come with many recommendations; but rather than be compensated with a share of how much that moves your bottom line, they'll take their enormously high hourly billing rates and be done, thank you very much.

Here is another warning sign. Like pigeons, Academics flock. They like safety in numbers and that, by flocking, any demand for Output is usually delayed. If you have an organization that regularly engages consultants for Vision and Process guidance, you might have a very wise Grunt, but more likely you have an Academic with a confidence problem.

To give credit where credit is due, many years ago I was on a corporate task force at Tektronix ("Tek"), where McKinsey had been brought in with a specific assignment to look at the problems of a particular product line. That division had been losing market share and had gone from being a cash cow to losing money. McKinsey did their thing and came back with some proposed solutions for the division; but they also came back with a larger issue. Essentially they said, "This product line is the least of your worries. You have much bigger problems corporate-wide," which they proceeded to outline. Now, you might say this was a brazen pitch to expand the consulting relationship, and probably it was.

But the issues they raised were very real, and their conclusions were accurate. Some of us Young Turks were rooting for them. When the senior executives decided to ignore the larger issues and simply thanked them for their work, the McKinsey team did something I've never seen anyone else have the guts to do. They sent a large wreath of black roses to the company with the note, "RIP Tektronix." Now, they had developed good personal relationships within the client, so the dark humor was not offensive (at least, not too much). But also there was a serious message there. It took quite a while, but all the chickens they identified ultimately came home to roost. Tek eventually suffered losses and layoffs, and finally was taken over. So, once again, Academics are not bad. In fact, none of these characters are bad in and by themselves. They just have to be properly used and properly balanced.

In the venture capital business, we see almost as many Academics as we do Dreamers and Brutes. In fact, our partnership has developed a rule: one tenured professor as part of a startup is a lot, and two is too many! Now, we actually don't see that many professors leaving the ivy-covered walls for the rough and tumble combat of business. But we do see many other Academics.

One of the most painful experiences with an Academic was a startup we backed based on technology that came out of one of the prestigious US national labs (a great place for Academics!). The inventor was a throwback: a classic tinkerer who appeared to have discovered a new way to harness motion to create electrical current by moving a magnet through a coil in a more efficient way.

We were impressed by what the technology could do, if it delivered as advertised, especially for soldiers in the field, who were carrying up to 40 pounds of batteries to power the myriad electronic systems now standard in combat. We saw the prototype system demonstrated repeatedly, and even engaged a well-respected professor from MIT to make sure the science was solid. (That may have compounded our mistake. We hired an Academic to tell us whether the Output of an Academic was likely to work!) The professor was so intrigued with the possibility that he too got caught up in the Vision and Process, while never fully vetting the Output.

After about a year of development, a problem was discovered showing that the technology had a fatal flaw. The Academic inventor was so committed to his approach that he couldn't let go of it, essentially refusing to believe the numbers he was seeing (and, in fact, hiding them for a while) because they didn't match his Vision and Process. We came perilously close to writing a second check. Fortunately, we hired a CEO who asked the right questions, looked at the real Output, and told us to save our breath and our money. It simply wasn't going to work.

One final war story from the Academic battlefield: We had a previously successful entrepreneur come to us with a radical idea for a software company. This individual had been quite successful in the Open Source field and felt the development model could be extended to the delivery model. He posited that large corporations would respond favorably to the idea that for the software they would usually have custom built, but which provided no competitive advantage (think compliance software for financial institutions), they could get the software built collectively with their competitors. The pitch was, "Work together with other industry heavyweights to specify what you all need. We'll then build it at a fraction of the price compared to what the larger enterprise software firms will charge you if you do it on your own." As a Vision, it made a lot of sense (we thought), and the approach of using Open Source development to create the products also made sense. Finally, the founder was wired into many large potential customers where this concept might get traction.

The problem was, those big customers just couldn't bring themselves to collaborate with their enemies, even if it made perfect sense economically. For them, the politics of telling their management that they were going to co-develop software with the guys trying to eat their lunch every day wasn't palatable.

Now, to be fair to this entrepreneur, he did try to adjust his Vision and Process and find Output someone would buy, and his firm managed to survive longer than his original premise would have allowed. But in the end, the company had to be labeled an Academic—long on Vision, long on Process, but completely missing the Output necessary to survive. And millions of dollars were lost.

Let me close this section with one of my favorite quotes on this subject, from Theodore Roosevelt:

> "It is not the critic who counts; not the man who points out how the strong man stumbles, or where the doer of deeds could have done them better. The credit belongs to the man who is actually in the arena, whose face is marred by dust and sweat and blood, who strives valiantly; who errs and comes short again and again; because there is not effort without error and shortcomings; but who does actually strive to do the deed; who knows the great enthusiasm, the great devotion, who spends himself in a worthy cause, who at the best knows in the end the triumph of high achievement and who at the worst, if he fails, at least he fails while daring greatly. So that his place shall never be with those cold and timid souls who know neither victory nor defeat."

The key is to get the Academics into that arena Roosevelt mentions, force them to get some dirt on their hands, or at a minimum team them up with some gladiators who relish a good fight.

THREE EASY STEPS TO IDENTIFY AN ACADEMIC

- Drive the conversation from "should do" to "have done." Academics use the word "should" more than anyone on the planet. This is how we *should* execute on our Vision. This is how we *should* have solved that problem. This is how we *should* do it differently next time. To be fair, such prescriptive advice can be useful. But it doesn't substitute for real accomplishment: "This is what we *have* done" statements are what you want to hear from people and groups who also care about their Output. Force Academics out of their comfort zone.

- Ask directly about their Output. In chapter six (The Bureaucrat), you'll read about what a new CEO at BIC Pens did to start making his people accountable for their Output to help meet the corporation's objectives. That technique will work for any character that lacks Output, not just Bureaucrats. If the department in question is a staff function, then ask how often their Output becomes the input other groups actually use to benefit the enterprise.

- Schedules in which the suspected Academic players have responsibility for Output are fuzzy or constantly slipping. Academics always have well-articulated reasons why the "when" part of their world needs to be put off. There is always a rationale for continuing to improve the product rather than being forced to call it "good enough" and end the development process—with all the attendant accountability. An engineering colleague of mine used to call this (inelegantly) "turd-polishing." For some, it feels safer to do that than to live with the consequences of shipping.

YOU'VE FOUND AN ACADEMIC, NOW WHAT?

As with all the other characters, Academics aren't "bad," they're just limited. If you want to take advantage of their strengths, you need to know how to leverage them while mitigating their inherent shortcomings. There are three basic steps you can take:

- Put them on the road. Academics benefit from getting close to customers, be they external or internal. Once they see how their ideas and Processes can matter in the real world, as long as they have Output to go with it, they find it much easier either to take the personal risk to be measured against that metric, or team with someone who does.

  You may recall a United Airlines commercial showing some business people sitting at a conference table with the boss, talking about how they'd just lost a key account they'd had for years, and it was time they all got face to face with their customers again. This was a company that apparently had fallen victim to Academic behavior. After the boss passed out the airline tickets to his direct reports, someone noticed he had one sticking out of his shirt pocket. "Where are you going?" he was asked. "To see that old client we just lost," he replied.

When I finished grad school, I was offered a job at Hewlett Packard. Their plan was to take freshly minted MBAs and stick them in customer support for 18 months, spending every day dealing with real customers and the real problems those people had with HP's products. While I didn't take that job, the thinking behind the corporate training model was sound. HP was blessed with many bright, visionary people and polished Processes. But they wanted to be sure no one confused those necessary ingredients with the need for high quality Output.

- Find a Grunt and convince the Academic to be their coach. Academics do get a charge out of seeing other people succeed based on their guidance. We all know teachers and coaches who revel in the progress and accomplishment of their students or players. In a funny way, this is where Academics actually have Output. If properly directed and focused, their Output can be helping to create others with successful Output.

- Make their world reflect the risk of the business. Many Academics are what they are because they are risk averse. If you can get them more comfortable with taking risk, they might just embrace Output as something they will accept, if not fully embrace. Perhaps start with baby steps. Make a small portion of the Academic's compensation dependent on some Output that is easily measured and not too difficult to achieve. Over time, raise the bar slowly and systematically.

YOUR PERSONAL ACADEMIC

Are you an Academic in your personal life? Are you risk averse? Or are you just lazy?

I was once in the audience in a corporate sales training seminar; the goal was to get the sales people to call higher in the customer's organization. The seminar leader (a consultant, and therefore probably an Academic himself!) challenged the audience this way:

"What would happen if you made a direct call to the CEO? What's the worst thing that could happen? You don't get past the executive assistant or you get a meeting but the CEO says 'no' to your proposal."

"So, then what's the worst thing that could happen? You miss your sales quota."

"So, then what's the worst thing that could happen? You get fired."

"So, then what's the worst thing that could happen? You can't get another job."

"So, then what's the worst thing that could happen? You run out of money."

"So, then what's the worst thing that could happen? You can't buy any food and you die."

"I have bad news for you today. We're all going to die!"

"So, you might as well call high!"

The laughter in the room helped break the ice by showing those sales people how ridiculous their fear of failure was when compared to the real issues at stake. Think about this for yourself and run through the same, "What am I scared about?" exercise. Failure in the rear view mirror is much smaller than it appeared. So, take the risk!

Maybe you need someone to help you with your Output—a Grunt, or a Merchant, or a Brute, or, best of all, a Success. The reason personal trainers exist, along with the host of other people dedicated to serving the needs of well-meaning procrastinators, is that we all can use a hand (or a shove) sometimes. Go find and/or hire one of those people. Help guide them towards your Vision, and then allow them to guide you to Output.

Finally, measure yourself on the "cocktail party expert" scale. Are you prone to sounding off about a multitude of topics, as long as the conversation can be limited to a few minutes and a few superficial sound bites of analysis and dogma? Some of this is fine, of course. It is the lubrication in our social interactions with people we don't know well. We expound on one subject until we run out of content, and then excuse ourselves to refresh our drinks. Many of us can wax eloquently on what our local sports teams "should" do differently, but few of us have the ability to get out and mix it up with the real players. I believe one of the reasons for the success of online fantasy sports leagues and multi-player video games is that they enable Academics to pretend they are Successes in some mythical realm. Don't get caught in that trap. Enjoy those pastimes if you like, but remember to focus back where real Output matters in your life.

FIVE

The Brute

"We will bury you!"

Nikita Khrushchev

Khrushchev as a leader was brutish. But the former Soviet Union also was a Brute. There is a significant difference. Brutish implies arrogant and belligerent. Being a Brute refers to a lack of sustainable Process competence.

The Soviet Union collapsed because, while it had a Vision (the socialist workers paradise) and Output (making it one of the two super military powers of the latter half of the twentieth century), it lacked a Process to regularly produce high quality products that met customer needs, other than the needs of their military (for a while). The Marxist slogan, "From each according to his ability, to each according to his needs," could not scale as human nature intervened.

Today we see Brutes of all sizes and shapes in organizational form. Every startup we've ever backed has been, essentially, a Brute. This is not a criticism, but a fact. All startups begin with the Vision of the founders, a tireless work ethic, and a dedication to producing something people will buy to keep the doors open. But it is also fair to say that Brutes are Peter Principals waiting to happen. No matter how compelling the Vision, no matter how exciting the Output (in the short term), ultimately Processes need to be put in place to make sure those high quality products keep coming, even after the founders get tired, or rich, or leave to found the next shiny startup. The key is to *see* the wall before you *hit* the wall, and then build a Process ramp *over* that wall.

The example I feel most personally again relates to Mentor Graphics in the 1980s. Mentor developed software to help electronics engineers produce chips and circuit boards. If ever there was a Brute that proved you can succeed in the short term, we were it. And the first manifestation of successful Brute behavior came very soon after we were founded. Our executive team was working on planning, customer contact and fund raising, while the engineers were slaving away at their keyboards. One day, quite unexpectedly, we were approached by one of the more senior members of the team, telling us in no uncertain terms that the engineers were ready to quit. We were stunned. We asked why. Because we had declined to buy them cots so they could sleep over at work while their software code was compiling, and also the lights in the parking lot were going out at 2AM and they were tripping while walking to their cars. These guys weren't just Brutes, they were Super Brutes! Needless to say, after a quick trip to the local camping store and a call to the landlord, everyone calmed down and went back to work. And work they did. One hundred hour weeks were the norm, not the exception.

Later on, I got myself into trouble with the spouse of one of these Super Brute software engineers. As the product started to come to life, it was my job to enlist Beta sites: companies that would dedicate their resources to banging on this immature code from our then unheard-of company. At 7:30 AM one morning in New Jersey I was preparing for a demonstration to RCA engineers. Now, Mentor Graphics was in Portland, Oregon, where the time was 4:30 AM. I tried and tried to get the as-yet-unreleased software to load on the computer, but it obstinately refused.

Finally, with no alternative, I called our lead systems engineer Rick at his home in Oregon. His wife Martha groggily answered the phone. "Hi Martha, it's Gerry. I'm really sorry to disturb you, but I'm on the East coast trying to give a demo and I can't get the Beta code to load. Can I talk to Rick please?" There was a long, awkward silence on the other end. Then she said, "Gerry, Rick's still at work, I think you should try him there." Click.

I never called anyone at home again without first checking at the office.

There were many other examples of Brute force success. Near the end of our first release of the code, it was clear that we needed to throw some features overboard to keep the release date from slipping. One Friday, we told that same Rick that his application would have to be deferred until a later release. On Monday, when we came in, the code of his that we'd chosen to delay was complete, and Rick was asleep on one of those previously acquired cots. No one was going to cancel or defer his project!

Some years later, I realized late one night before a crack-of-dawn flight that I'd left something vital at the office, so I departed early to swing by Mentor and pick it up. But when I arrived, there was a problem. I had a key, but no idea what the security code was on the alarm. Until then, I had never been to the office at any time, day or night, weekday or weekend, when there wasn't someone working. I'd never bothered to learn the code because our culture of Brutes didn't require me to.

Now, as you hear about these tales of heroism, you need to reflect on heroes as a class of people. How many do you know? How long do they seem to continue to operate as heroes?

The problem is that heroes don't scale!

If you have a Rick, or a Ginger, or a whole group of such type-A, brilliant, hard-working Brutes, congratulations. They are the stuff of legend. But they are not the stuff of longevity. At some point, they will get tired, they will burn out, they will get bored, or they will be recruited away. And then you are stuck with a hero culture in a decidedly un-heroic world. You had better be laying down the sustainable Processes and backfilling the talent you need long before you hit the Brute barrier, the Peter Principal of all business behaviors.

Let me share how dangerous Brute culture can be, drawing again from the Mentor Graphics history book. When it came time to step up to a full second-generation software system for our customers, almost a decade after those initial heroes launched the first products, our engineers (now numbering 800 rather than that initial team of eight) begged me to allow them the time and money to put in place the development tools (the Processes) necessary to manage and complete such a daunting task.

I refused. I still remembered the days of old when the founding team could be heroes and accomplish the impossible. Burned into my brain was the notion that Brute behavior could always be called upon to lift us up by our bootstraps. The result: $100 million of losses, based on the delays of that second generation software, and traced directly to the success we had had years earlier. Brutes (unlike Mr. Khrushchev) and their successes are seductive. Don't be taken in.

As I wrote at the beginning of this chapter, almost every startup is a Brute. In fact, many new product lines and divisions in large companies are, too. But they are Brutes only in comparison with their heavily Process-laden sister groups. Compared to true startups, they can actually look like Process-heavy Bureaucrats. This, then, is one of the great dilemmas of corporate management. How do you create the vitality of a startup, the work ethic, the passion, and the creativity without saddling it with the long term sustainable Processes to ensure it won't hit the wall? But, how can you ignore the Processes that assure your corporate quality and reliability goals, and not risk customer satisfaction and brand damaging disasters?

For a complete answer, you'll need to read chapter ten (The Success). For now, let's just say that there are times when you actually do have to choose deliberately where and when to take your risk. For lunch today we're serving Innovation or Process, but not both. Being a Brute, or any one of the less than successful characters, is not a death sentence as long as you know where you are, who you are, and why you are there at that time. Brutes that know they need to add Process are Successes in the making.

One of the ways this gets brought home to those of us in the venture capital business is when we are entertaining acquisition offers from large industrial enterprises for one of our portfolio companies. We often hear comments such as:

> "We are amazed at how much you have accomplished with such a small team in such a short time. But, looking forward, there is no way we can take the products you still have in development and finish them under the schedule you have proposed with the resources you have planned. It will take twice as long with double the staff. Once we factor that in, and our corporate overhead, your product lines don't look all that profitable to us."

Now, think about it. What this big company just said was, "We want your innovation, because without it we can't grow. But once we burden it with our bureaucracy and Process, we can't make money."

There's got to be a better way. And, in fact, there is.

Large corporations need to learn how to create and/or acquire Brutes, and then assimilate them carefully into the enterprise so the sustainable Processes get layered in slowly enough not to disrupt the advantages of Brutes, but not so slowly as to risk customer backlash. Is this hard? You bet! But it is immeasurably harder if you don't appreciate that's what you need to do and so you either leave the Brute to its inevitable problems with Process, or brute-force it (sorry) into the maw of mother corporation and kill the innovation. Many have argued that one of the distinctive core competencies of technology giant Cisco was its ability to acquire, integrate, and yet not suffocate innovative teams. It is hard to name another company so firmly fixed on this skill as a key success factor. For most others, it is either haphazard or anecdotal. For Cisco, it was a successful value system, although one they seemed to lose for a while. If your large enterprise really wants to grow via acquisition, and views its targets as young dynamic teams, you need to be able to understand what makes Brutes tick, and then how not to stop time when you appear at the door. The best and simplest way, of course, is to keep these teams as separate divisions or business units.

BACK TO SCHOOL

Brutes are not limited to the for-profit sector of business by any means. I once served on a local school board during a very stressful time. The state legislature in Oregon passed a law designed to save money by consolidating school districts. Until then, school systems could exist as K-8 programs, sending their students to other nearby districts for high school, with state dollars following the child. The state decided this was inefficient, and so the law said every district had to offer a full K-12 program. So, those K-8 only districts faced a choice: consolidate into an adjacent district that already had a high school program (the goal of the law) or create a high school.

Our little residential district was one of those K-8 only programs, with the kids going to a nearby high school, and a fine one at that. But that town next door had the more common K-6, junior high, high school structure, while we were very wedded to our K-8 model and to the small class sizes and extra programs. So, we decided to create an academically-focused high school, even though the size of our community dictated it would be much smaller than traditional American high schools: no more than 300 students at capacity. Fortunately, we had a superintendent who was a very effective Brute to get us started.

The first order of business was to find a site, which was no small task given that our community was zoned exclusively residential. So, we had to look outside our district boundaries and had to do so very quickly or fall prey to the new law. Our superintendent found an abandoned school in Portland and arranged for a short term lease. The school opened with days to spare, having quietly ignored the requirement to get city land use approval to reopen. That's classic Brute behavior, by the way. "Better to beg forgiveness than ask for permission."

Our Brute of a superintendent had saved the day, and continued to do so by getting the school moved a year later to a second temporary location at a local university before the bureaucrats in Portland discovered our lack of building use approval at the first location. A few years later, we finally found a permanent site that fit the bill. It was an old school, again, but this time we would get official land use approval, and do a multi-million dollar renovation to the facility before moving in. That was when our superintendent found himself (and we as board members joined him) on the wrong side of Brute behavior.

He was terrific doing the emergency, save-the-day work to keep us independent and moving forward. But he was not prepared to manage a multi-million dollar construction project, with all the complex processes one needs to keep such a project on budget. We opened on time, but then were shocked to get the final bill for about two million dollars more than voters had authorized in our school bond. We fell into the classic trap of worshiping our Brute "hero" who had gotten us through the tough times, but not recognizing that the context had changed, and we needed a different Process skill to take the next step successfully.

THREE EASY STEPS TO IDENTIFY A BRUTE

- Ask "how." When you see a person or an organization brimming with Vision and hitting all their Output targets, ask about their Processes. Investigate the "how" before celebrating the "what." What you often will find is that the first answers are, on the surface, comforting. "Oh, we have it down to a system …", which is then followed by anecdotal descriptions of people doing extraordinary things. Go back to the definition in chapter two and take each key phrase and investigate how well the person or organization in question measures up to that benchmark:

*"The structures, methods and procedures
to repeatedly produce timely, high quality
products or services, independent of changes
in personnel."*

- Drive for specifics. Often it is easy for those inside Brute organizations to brush off questions about "structures, methods and procedures," since to them the way things are done is just "known." But when pressed for specific examples, or asked why something is done one way versus a potential alternative, they are at a loss for words. An easy way to think about this is: any Process that cannot be described crisply suffers from one of two fatal flaws. It is either living in someone's head, and if that someone goes away you fail the "independent of changes in personnel" test; or, it is really not a Process at all but more a more random series of events that seems to work but is subject to variation, and then you fail the "repeatedly" test.

- Substitute players. You may not want to do this for real right away, but you can certainly run a scenario with your team asking, "What if Sally, the guru of 'x', were to leave tomorrow? What would we do? How well would we perform starting the next day?" This is not to say that every superstar in the organization must have a fully functioning backup in place. Most companies don't have the luxury of that depth. But you can determine how much of a hero culture you have in this Brute-like group. The more you have, the more risky your position.

YOU'VE FOUND A BRUTE, NOW WHAT?

As mentioned earlier, a Brute is a Peter Principal-bound organization on a direct path to hit a wall. You need to take advantage of the positives of the Brute, but also you need to build a ramp over that wall before you hit it. There are three basic steps you can take:

- Start talking about the risk of hitting the wall. Sure, you will get resistance and pushback. You'll hear people complain, "Here comes the bureaucracy!" But once the initial emotion subsides, most people will agree to take some small steps. Ask what things can be done to improve (or create) Processes, yet not bog down progress. I've found that even the worst Brute actually will appreciate a little Process care and feeding—especially if they help create those Processes.

- Look for complementary pairings. By now, this prescription sounds repetitive, and it is. But if you have some Academics, Merchants, or open-minded Bureaucrats (yes, they do exist) in the organization, think about ways to link them with your Brute in a constructive way.

For all the bad press given to "task forces" and "tiger teams," I've seen them work wonders in this area. The key is to get the make-up of the team right from the start. Most companies correctly comprise these teams of people from different organizations, but do not worry about comprising them of different characters. Add that dimension to the team, and then charge them with putting together a "Success" model, and you have taken a major step in the right direction.

- Get started on succession planning. You may not be able to have a bona fide backup for any of your heroes in the short term, but at least now you know who they are, and what functions they perform. Single them out for recognition, and then enlist their support in finding potential junior people they can help train and guide to take their place someday. Most Super Brutes I've known appreciate the recognition, and the responsibility this gives them.

YOUR PERSONAL BRUTE

Are you a Brute in your personal life? Do you have a list of things you'd like to accomplish in your career, your family, your health, your personal activities, but never seem to get beyond a few steps in the right direction before giving up?

It turns out major industries are standing by to help

you and/or take advantage of your Brutishness. You know those weight-loss program, exercise equipment and quit smoking commercials that crop up every December and January? They play to the Brute in all of us. We may have a consistent Vision of health improvement, but that's usually all. Then, as a New Year's resolution, we get some temporary Output (making us temporary Brutes) with the help of an equally temporary Process like a crash diet or a few weeks at the gym. However, unless we commit to a sustainable Process, we quickly fall back to our old habits. One study indicated that if you get past 90 days with a new personal Process, you may have successfully changed your behavior in a permanent way and so actually be on the way to success.

Remember Ginger Brooks in chapter one? She was a smart woman with a constant to-do list. And as she crossed off some items, others found their way onto the list. She had Output, and had some Vision about what she needed and wanted to do. But the very fact that that list was "task oriented" rather than "Process oriented" limited her to short term goals versus any long term Vision. Now, there is nothing wrong with a to-do list. Just don't confuse it with a Process for future success, unless the items on it are things you are doing to improve yourself over time, rather than trying to get them all crossed off your list by Thursday.

So, what can you do to get by this basic blocking function of human nature?

- Make a second to-do list, a long term one. On this one, start with a goal or two and a description of the Output that, if sustained, would tell you that success was at hand. Now write down some possible processes you would have to master to achieve that sustained success.

- For each Process, write a to-do list for that. What do you have to do differently, or learn, or get better at? How are you going to make that happen over a period of time longer than is usual for you to stick to something hard and new? For all the aspersions cast earlier in this book about Steven Covey's *7 Habits of Highly Effective People,* here you have a perfect application of "begin with the end in mind" and take time to "sharpen the ax."

Recall that in chapter one Henry Long labeled himself a Brute when it came to his painting. He was probably being a little harsh on himself. He had committed to taking painting classes to improve his Process. He had the roadmap in place to becoming a Success in that dimension of his life. Even if his motivation was a little suspect, given his attraction to Ginger Brooks, he was doing the right thing. In fact, therein lies an interesting observation. Henry had found some adjacent motivation to help him stick with the hard part of shifting from a Brute to a Success. That's a good idea. Anything that will help you get past that 90 day wall is worth latching onto. People who exercise successfully with friends find the social interaction makes the hard part of the Process more palatable.

Almost everyone I've ever known is a Brute in their personal life at some level (myself included). So, again, that is not a condemnation as much as it is both a fact and a challenge. Highly successful people find ways to take their fuzzy Vision of personal growth, reduce it to steps they need to take, and then systematically take those steps. It may not be a straight path. It may be one where occasionally it is two steps forward and one back. But sticking to the path and measuring your progress against that long term to-do list will give you a great opportunity to achieve your goals, personally and professionally.

SIX

The Bureaucrat

"You can lead a bureaucrat to water, but you can't make him think."

Ric Keller

There is a story about a new executive who was brought into BIC Pen's US operation to turn around floundering performance and a bloated organization. He told all the employees to provide him an 8½ x 11 handwritten piece of paper describing their "Output" by 5 PM the following day. The next day here's what happened:

- Those that missed the 5 PM deadline were fired.
- Those who typed their responses were fired.
- Those who turned in more than one page were fired.
- Those who could not describe their Output were fired.
- For the rest, the new leader looked at their Output and decided whether to keep them or not.

In one fell swoop, he cut through an organization that

had become a classic Bureaucrat to make it crystal clear that instructions were to be followed and that Output mattered. The organization moved quickly from being a Bureaucrat to acting more like a Merchant (see chapter seven). While that did not ensure ultimate success, it at least got things headed in a positive direction. Long term, the organization still needed Vision, and Process could not disappear. But, in the short term, no one confused the means to an end with an end in itself.

When you reach chapter eleven, you'll find another issue with Bureaucrats. Sometimes they are just misunderstood. Their view of how they fit into the Vision for the enterprise and how they measure Output may be somewhat different than others, yet still vital. So, before you make them walk the plank, make sure that you have all the nautical charts needed to continue the voyage without them. In that last chapter, you'll find a finance department that is viewed by others as a Bureaucrat, when in fact their Vision (predictable earnings for Wall Street) and their Output (an attractive stock price) are both things the rest of the company can appreciate. But perhaps because the conversation has not taken place between them and the other functional departments, no one gives them credit for that.

More often though, when you find a Bureaucrat, you have found a real problem to be addressed. One of the activities in the government sector I wholeheartedly applaud is the notion of a sunset provision on laws. It forces the Bureaucrats (the legislators) to review whether the laws (the Processes and rules) they put in place still make sense. In many cases, the world moves on and the regulations are no longer needed. In others, the law of unintended consequences makes the situation worse than it was before. Sunset provisions force scrutiny on both fronts.

In the business world there are no such constructs in place. Once a Process or rule enters the enterprise it's there for good, unless a tremendous force is applied to remove or modify it. The law of inertia applies in spades in a corporate setting. As with governments, rules and regulations beget organizations which develop constituencies, budgets and political clout. They "do not go gentle into that good night." (Thank you, Dylan Thomas)

In my role as an operating executive, more than once I was confronted with a complaint that some Process or rule was "stupid," only to be countered by a Bureaucrat who replied, "But that's the way we've always done it." Ultimately, I had to issue my own rule: "The old rules may be good rules, or maybe not anymore. If you think we are doing something stupid just because we always have, you need to speak up." I'm realistic enough to know that didn't solve the problem entirely. But it did embolden a few brave souls to challenge the status quo and get more efficient, or perhaps fewer, Processes in place.

Later, I discovered that some in the organization liked to use my name as the ultimate way to handle objections. They would say, "Gerry said we should do this, or do it that way, or not do it the way you are suggesting." Of course, in a large organization few people knew what I actually had said (if anything) on the subject and even fewer would think to challenge my "wisdom." In a sense, others in the company made me into the ultimate Bureaucrat, without my knowledge.

Finally I'd had enough and wrote an article for the

company newsletter titled "Gerry Said," in which I laid bare the fallacy of the approach people were using. I told the rank and file a few simple things:

> "I don't say that much about the things people say I do. I don't understand the details as well as most of you, especially those closest to the action in your area of expertise. And even if I did say 'that,' there's a decent chance I was wrong. So, the next time someone shuts you down with a 'Gerry Said,' feel free to push back at them, or come directly to me and ask about it."

I don't recall anyone ever taking me up on the last offer, but it did seem to stop my being used as the uber-Bureaucrat. Be careful that isn't being done by folks in your organization.

A human resources organization in a firm I once worked for had a formal rule. You could not hire anyone unless the job had first been posted internally for three weeks. That Process was sensible; it helped motivate employees because they had first crack at all advancement opportunities. It also cost us an absolutely critical employee, whose company announced they were being taken over by a large, bureaucratic organization. Our firm knew of this person through interaction at technical conferences and knew he was, literally, one of the best in his field. He contacted one of his peers in our company as soon as the acquisition was announced, indicating he'd be putting his resume on the street the next day. Everyone knew he'd be snatched up in a heartbeat. We had no current opening for such a person, because in fact we didn't think we had any chance of attracting one of the handful of rock stars in that domain. But now we might. And we had no budget for that job either.

As you might expect, HR said that we'd have to post the job for three weeks before we could talk to this person. And Finance said we'd have to get a budget waiver from the CEO to hire above the expense plan.

And we said, "You people don't understand how precious and perishable this candidate is!"

And no one listened. By the time we'd jumped through the corporate Bureaucracy hoops to get approval to hire and letting internal candidates apply, a much more nimble company had snatched up that genius. Later, he helped develop a product line that gobbled our market share in large bites. The lesson was: Yes, there are sensible rules for everything. But if you let the Bureaucrats own the enterprise, they will. And their Processes will become not a means, but an end.

More recently, I was involved in a situation where we had a struggling startup and began to feel we needed a new CEO. I was having dinner the night before a board meeting with one of the other investors when he mentioned that a certain local executive with world class experience at a large company, and also successful startup stripes on his sleeve, was looking for a new challenge. I almost jumped across the table to hug my fellow VC. (Note: This does not happen much in the venture capital industry!)

But when I brought the opportunity to the board the

next day (in executive session with the current CEO not in the room), I got pushback.

> "Gerry, we agree that we need a change at the top. But shouldn't we do a national or international search to make sure we get the best candidate? This person you mention sounds great, but he's a little short on experience in our specific niche."

They essentially wanted to put the usual (and usually smart) Process in place on this key activity.

However, my response was, for me, unusually forceful.

> "This person is as good, and probably better, than anyone we are going to get through a search process. We need a new leader now, and he's available now, right here. We're not in Silicon Valley, where executives like this grow on trees. Getting the perfect person, with the perfect background, who will locate to this city, is a dicey process. This company may die while we do things the 'normal' way. Sometimes a rare opportunity lands in your lap and one just did. We need to hire him now!"

To the credit of the other board members, they heard

me and we proceeded to bring on the new CEO. In less than two years, the company went from shrinking revenues to doubling in size, and from losing money to profitability.

Now, the story of ignoring Process to act boldly in the moment doesn't always end this well, but it does go to show that Bureaucrats come in many forms. My fellow board members rarely would be described that way. They are each successful business people who have grown firms both small and large, and on other topics they have been anything but "Process bound." Yet, we all need to be alert to not letting Process keep us from achieving the result we all want.

THREE EASY STEPS TO IDENTIFY A BUREAUCRAT

- This one can be the easiest of all to unmask. If it is within your organization, other groups will be all too ready to identify the Bureaucrat for you, usually by that name. You will hear lots of wailing about how the Bureaucrat's "rules and regulations" are stifling innovation and productivity. If it is your sales organization complaining, they'll tag the Bureaucrat with the reason they missed plan last quarter. On the other hand, if your whole enterprise has become a Bureaucrat, you'll see that evidenced in poor Output results coupled with increased justification why that actually is good for the company, because you are "sticking to your corporate values about quality," or some such talk.

- Pretend to eliminate the organization/ function. Run an exercise in your mind imagining that tomorrow the Bureaucrat was gone and not replaced. What would happen to the company? How long would it take to impact those farther down your internal supply chain? If your answer is that things would immediately get worse, then maybe you don't have a Bureaucrat but rather an intelligent Process in place. But, if you think things would get better immediately and then take a while, if ever, to get worse, you have a true Bureaucrat.

- Ask the question, "So what?" of the person or group. Force the organization to justify their existence. It may be that your view is too limited. Perhaps you don't fully appreciate what this group accomplishes. By forcing them to explain their raison d'être, you will improve your perspective and force them to be more introspective.

YOU'VE FOUND A BUREAUCRAT, NOW WHAT?

You may recall how Henry Long suggested, "Don't burn 'em, turn 'em." Start with the notion that the Processes embraced by the Bureaucrat may well be essential. What you need is to get them working for you, not against you. Then, and only then, take a step back and think about whether

you've become too Process–bound and how you might relax some of those "rules."

- Figure out what makes the Bureaucrat happy
  or makes their life easier, as contractor
  Rodriguez did for Burt Johnson in chapter
  one. As with any of us, once you make my life
  flow more smoothly, I'm much more likely
  to listen when you ask me to take on more
  complexity. Adding Vision and/or Output
  emphasis to a Bureaucrat definitely ratchets up
  their complexity coefficient, so first help them
  be ready to accept it.
- Educate them on how their role matters in the
  organization, and at the same time how the
  team needs some flexibility to react to changes
  in requirements, or schedules, or customer
  demands or competitive threats. While I
  haven't seen too many Bureaucrats jump all
  the way to Success mode, the better ones can
  at least appreciate the value of Vision and
  Output and adjust.
- Team them with a Brute, while keeping a close
  eye that they don't kill each other in the short
  term. Many years ago I was in an executive
  role where we had a classic Brute of a product
  development team that had started to do poor
  quality work as it grew from a handful of
  people to over one hundred. We put a terrific
  quality assurance person into the mix, with
  authority to act, and for a while it looked like

Armageddon had ensued. The Brutes objected mightily to the new Processes, while the Bureaucrat was driven to distraction by the ad hoc nature of the Brutes' approach. However, through a lot of talk and late night pizza, détente finally was reached. The Bureaucrat grudgingly agreed to modify his strict rules a bit, and the Brutes grudgingly agreed to adhere to the new scaled-back rules, at least most of the time. The result was a couple of years of remarkably high Output both in quantity and quality from that organization.

YOUR PERSONAL BUREAUCRAT

Are you a Bureaucrat in your personal life? The easiest way to know is to ask yourself how many times you justify (or, more likely, constrain) what you are going to do about something by the word "should." Unlike the "should" warning in chapter four (The Academic), this one relates not to how to achieve a specific Vision, but to some ethereal "how one should be." This is the way I "should" do things. This is how I "should" feel, or act, or think. Bureaucrats are rule-bound, and the word "should" in the "how you should be" context is a rule-oriented command. And those rules almost always are not real, but imagined.

How many times have we read about people pigeon-holed in their mundane corporate jobs for years who finally take the leap to paint, or teach, or sail around the world, only to find that the barriers to doing what they loved versus what they "should" do were only in their heads the whole time?

No one can tell you how you should live your life. That's a journey we all take on our own. Of course, there are social norms to consider and laws to obey, but those usually are far less restrictive than the limits we put on ourselves. There is a great line from an old Eagles song: "So often times it happens that we live our lives in chains. And we never even know we have the key."

You have the key. Turn it!

Take a step back and think about what you would enVision your life to be if you were "free" to act as you'd like. Now take a look forward and imagine the Output you'd be creating or be responsible for. Then think hard about what is holding you back and what Process you could change to get from "I should" to "I want to" to "I can" to "I will," and eventually "I am!"

SEVEN

The Merchant

"A merchant who approaches business with the idea of serving the public well has nothing to fear from competition."

J.C. Penney

Mr. Penney was correct in the world that he knew then, where serving the public did not change very much from year to year. If he just kept doing what he had always done he'd be fine. But in today's world, it doesn't hold true any longer.

We visit Merchants every day. They have very well-polished Processes for getting their products into their stores in an optimized way, and they stand ready to deliver whatever it is we want, as long as what we want is essentially the same thing we've wanted for a while. Merchants often compete on price, because it turns out once someone is a successful Merchant, the road to commoditization—or worse, replacement by a new aggressive competitor—is not far behind.

Years ago, I was doing a consulting project for Outboard Marine Corp (OMC)—the company that manufactured Johnson and Evinrude outboard motors. They were starting to see erosion in their market position in Europe from Japanese companies Honda and Yamaha, and wanted to figure out what was happening and what they should do about it.

In my interviews with boat and motor retailers in England and Scotland, an interesting trend appeared. It seems the OMC 9.9hp motors had been experiencing some serious quality problems, although the rest of the product line was solid. The 9.9hp motor was the highest volume outboard being sold in the UK at the time. The Japanese firms had figured all this out and had quickly initiated new design and automated manufacturing for just that one motor—while OMC kept their old Processes, their fully depreciated manufacturing lines, and old not-so-great design in place. Honda and Yamaha offered their 9.9hp motors to the dealers as a way to keep their historical customers happy, but did not try to compete with OMC in any other product category. And OMC, with a limited Vision, saw no potentially fatal threat.

After a couple of years, with increasing success, the Japanese then offered those same dealers a 15hp motor. OMC had a reliable product there, but the Japanese firms understood that many motor buyers started small and traded up. Having had a good experience at 9.9hp, those customers opted to stay brand loyal as they moved to larger horsepower motors. Also, the UK dealers by now were comfortable with the new Japanese brands. So when, a few years later, the Japanese suddenly launched a full line of products in England, the dealers were delighted to take them on. OMC was caught as a Merchant in a rapidly changing world. And that grand old firm, founded by Ole Evinrude in 1907, didn't quite make it to the century mark, finally declaring bankruptcy in the year 2000.

For many, many years, Outboard Marine was a Success. They had about 66% market share in boat motors in the United States (the other third going to Mercury). They had a unique branding proposition, in which Johnson and Evinrude motors were identical under the cowling, giving them terrific manufacturing economies of scale, while they still managed to differentiate those brands in the eyes of the consumer. In the US, they had created a distribution model that gave local franchises exclusive rights to sell Evinrude or Johnson. In return, dealers agreed not ever (and I mean *ever*) to sell a motor from another vendor. So they faced almost no real competition.

OMC essentially had created a "protected market" via its own success, just as in chapter one our Merchant, Patrick Kelly, had a protected market from Walmart due to geography. And if you'd been a senior manager at OMC in the days when I was doing that consulting project, I'll bet there was a clearly defined, well understood Vision for the company.

The problem was, OMC's vision did not fully take into account the issue of "competitive leadership over time." They became complacent in their success and left a crack open for a challenger to gain a foothold. But because that challenger was not in their primary US market, at first they didn't recognize the seriousness of the threat. Later, as the Japanese firms gained market share in Europe, OMC didn't have the exclusive distribution power to stop them as they did in the US. Then the Japanese firms used their own power of distribution to align their new outboard motor sales with their historical US motorcycle and lawn mower outlets. Suddenly, OMC's protected market was protected no more. If the company had crafted a Vision that recognized both its strengths and its potential weaknesses earlier, they might have survived.

A similar story can be told about another fabulously successful company, Microsoft. Its incredible rise to dominance in personal computer software gave it a protected market in the 1980s and early 1990s. But, with the rise of the Internet, suddenly they found themselves in a position unlike the commanding one they had come to enjoy. They had become a Merchant, with great Process and outstanding Output in the form of profits, but with a Vision that was not sustainable against an array of new competitors playing by new rules. To the credit of Bill Gates, his challenge to his team in 1996 to "embrace and extend" allowed them to re-craft their Vision to include the Internet and continue to be successful. For all the stones thrown at Microsoft, many of which are well deserved, in this instance they deserve kudos.

Some fifteen years later, Microsoft once again had fallen into Merchant behavior as the technology winds shifted. In 2013, the company tried to modify their Vision to embrace the rise of mobile computing and cloud architectures. Time will tell if Microsoft can adopt a third Vision and again move back into full Success mode. It will be difficult, at best.

Besides shifting competitive behavior, a trigger event

can make a Success into a Merchant: a change in Vision driven not by evolving technology or new competition, but by dramatically broadened scope. We fell into this trap at Mentor Graphics. In fact, my Harvard Business Review article, *The Vision Trap*, talks about it in exactly those terms. While the article was written decades ago, its principles remain valid.

In Mentor's case, we created our own "protected market" by winning with our initial Vision and against initial competitors. However, unlike OMC, rather than get complacent we got arrogant. If we could win in the business segment in which we started (software for the design of electronic circuits), why couldn't we also win in other segments, like mechanical design? Or software design? Or document management? Rather than consolidating the gains we made by winning in the electronics segment, and being on the alert for potential rule-changing competitors, we wandered off into new areas in which we were not as likely to succeed as we thought. We were attracted to the next shiny object, and these new objects looked much shinier to us.

Over time, we noticed two things were happening. One set of competitors realized that, by themselves, they didn't have the scale to compete successfully with us in our core space. But each had a best-of-breed product which, if offered with the others, could be formidable. From that brainstorm Cadence Design was formed. And they ultimately ate our lunch. But we had ample opportunity to stop them, because we were in a position to acquire two of their three primary product lines before they joined forces. However, because our Vision didn't force us to play both offense and defense, but rather had us playing "across the fence" in other fields (and far from home), we didn't prioritize those potential deals highly enough and they were not made.

Then, as they did for Microsoft, the technology winds shifted. In our case it was the rise of "synthesis," with which engineers could describe their new designs in language form rather than capturing them as schematic diagrams. A firm called Synopsys appeared, with a terrific product. We responded with a weak one, a sort of placeholder that said to the market, "Me too" rather than, "We get it." And the market voted with their dollars for Synopsys.

Mentor Graphics became a Merchant by becoming distracted from its primary customer. So, while the Processes and Output were there for a while, and we enjoyed perhaps our best results on Wall Street during those times, the cancer had entered the body. It was only a matter of time before it spread.

FOUR EASY STEPS TO IDENTIFY A MERCHANT

If Bureaucrats are one of the easiest to identify, Merchants can be the hardest. On the surface, they look very much like a Success. We can all measure their Output, we can witness their Processes. But Vision is much harder to get your arms around, and some nice words on a PowerPoint slide can obfuscate the fact that the "emperor has no clothes."

- Ask about how you might be living in a protected market, be it real or imagined, what the threats are that could upset that position, and what their Vision is to deal with those possible threats. This focuses the conversation back on "competitive leadership over time" versus "look how well we are doing right now."

- They can tell you "what" they are doing but not "why." The "why" question forces the issue on where they think they are going. And from that, it allows you to probe into the Vision that is being followed and decide whether it meets all the criteria of the definition in chapter two. If not, you have a good place to start the conversation about how they might have become "Merchant-ized."

- Their goals are all short term. Again, Merchants look just like Successes based on Output. So if all you are measuring is the short term, you have a problem. Delve into the intermediate and longer term goals and then test them against customer needs and potential competitive strategies.

- They dismiss new ideas or potential competitive threats with, "Give me an example of someone else who has done that successfully." If you'd asked the people at OMC about how a Japanese competitor might enter their market in a distant geography with a single product, and then mapped out how they might use that beachhead to launch a full scale attack worldwide, they might well have been dismissive. The same might have been true at Microsoft when Netscape launched their Internet browser. But if the senior staff had been alert enough to run a few of those possible scenarios, they would have been faster to react when trouble came calling.

YOU'VE FOUND A MERCHANT, NOW WHAT?

Not only is a Merchant the hardest to identify, Merchants are usually the hardest to get to accept their position and therefore accept the need to change. They are meeting all their corporate goals, and being well rewarded for doing so. Usually, they need to get a punch in the nose in terms of Output before they will react. So, help them notice that their nose is being punched. Bill Gates did that when he called into question Microsoft's ability to compete with the new wave of Internet technology, and then issued his "embrace and extend" memo.

- Force a new "Visioning" process on the organization. Make them look at the world as it will be, not as it has been or it is now. For as much as I hate the phrase, "Think outside the box," it does lead people to look beyond their narrow view of the world to what might happen and where they might be vulnerable. I once led an executive offsite where we did this by breaking into cross-functional teams; each team had to create a fictitious new company that would compete with us, and then describe how they'd launch their initial attack, and proceed to take more of our turf. It was very instructive!

- Force a much deeper "lost sales" report on the group. Now, "sales" doesn't always mean the Sales department. But, making people talk to customers (those in their internal or external supply chain) very specifically about what they need, what they are getting (or not), and where they are looking to get what they aren't getting from your group. To be fair, OMC should be credited because that's exactly what they did in hiring the consulting firm where I was working. The bad news was, having seen the report from the consultants, they didn't have the sense of urgency to "embrace and extend" and react to it in a way that could have saved them.

- As always, teaming complementary characters can produce useful results. If you have some particularly wise and credible Dreamers in your midst, foist them on your resident Merchant. The cross pollination just may benefit both.

YOUR PERSONAL MERCHANT

Are you a Merchant in your personal life? Just as it is hard to identify a Merchant in the corporate world, it's hard to identify, or admit, that you are one in your life outside the workplace.

Personal Merchants have the same feeling of comfort that corporate ones do. You are enjoying your Output, you can point proudly to the Processes that get you there, and you might even be able to mouth convincing words about your personal Vision for your future.

So ask yourself, "Am I ready for dramatic changes? What would they look like? How would I react?"

Certainly we all have to accept that whatever our jobs are, they can be transient. If tomorrow you found yourself out of work, are you ready for that? Have you done the financial planning and saving to survive for some time on a meager income? Have you done the networking in advance of needing it so that you'd be ready to search for a new assignment, and have people eager to talk to you?

In my role as a venture capitalist, I am regularly approached by former entrepreneurs who say, "My board just decided that they want to make a change in my position, and I've been so heads down I haven't really established a network to help me find my next gig."

In the personal world, like the corporate one, you have to have a Vision that can handle change and challenge to the status quo. I got some great advice on the financial front many years ago, right after Mentor Graphics went public. Our stock broker said to me, "Do you want to eat well or sleep well? If you want to sleep well, after you pay off your student loans, let's set you up with a laddered bond portfolio." (To which I replied, "What's that?") On the downside, I missed most of the market boom in the 1990s. On the other hand, when the Internet bubble burst in 2000-2001, and the market melted down in 2008, I didn't feel nearly so bad. I slept well. He helped me with a personal Vision that

I would have messed up on my own.

EIGHT

The Grunt

"Grunt: A term of affection used to denote that filthy, sweaty, dirt-encrusted, footsore, camouflage-painted, tired, sleepy beautiful little son of a bitch who has kept the wolf away from the door for over two hundred years."

H. G. Duncan

Grunts are OK. No, really. Grunts make the world go around. They do all those things that we rely on and can't or won't do for ourselves: they deliver your newspaper, they clean up after you, and they stand midnight lookout duty on the ramparts. Grunts are the unseen heroes in the economy. But Grunts as organizations are deadly. They appear to be just fine in the short-term. Everyone works hard, and business goes on, and as long as absolutely nothing changes, all is well. But the day that anything disturbs the status quo, they fail.

You often see turnaround executives get paid fabulous amounts of money to be Grunts. They come into a floundering business and just pound on Output for a year, and, low and behold, sell more stuff after all. But shortly after they get the big bonus check, things begin to unravel. And the turnaround guys are off to the next assignment, while the company, now exhausted, dies.

Years ago, there was an individual who came to work in my company with great energy and a positive attitude. We were growing at an exponential rate and we desperately needed someone to take care of the customer support responsibilities. He was our first employee in that function, and he did a terrific job—at least at the start. We gave him very clear instructions about what we expected, and he performed. As we grew, we made him manager of the department, which he began to staff.

Over time, as our customer base grew, we noticed that this group was not performing the way we had hoped and customers were complaining. But there was no question that our manager had his heart in the right place. He just didn't have the skills for a job that had become much more complex. We let him know we needed to make a change, but that we valued him highly, just not in that role. As a terrific, loyal Grunt, he took the news well, and dove into the next position we gave him. It was another key area, but with less complexity and no people management responsibility. He again performed well until the company's growth drove the complexity of that role too high and he began to struggle. So we made another change, narrowing his role while still retaining this wonderful employee. This was someone who could take on any challenge and give it his all. He wasn't a Brute, because he was not able to internalize, much less generate, any meaningful Vision. But he would put all his energy into whatever we asked him to do.

This Grunt's story has a happy ending, by the way. By checking his ego at the door, and accepting roles where he could succeed and help the enterprise, he ended up staying at the company for many years. And those stock options he got in the early days? Let's just say he lives VERY comfortably today. Once again, none of these characters are "bad"; you just have to deal with them properly by understanding which character they are.

In the venture capital industry, one type of Grunt is called a "crab." Crabs are companies that at one time had a Vision that faded away over time. They may or may not have ever developed Process, but it is gone too. All they have left is Output. They skitter sideways down the beach of business, not growing revenues, but eating cash as they go. As investors, they drive us crazy. They usually are too established simply to walk away from, because they are real businesses with real customers. But, because they still require cash to stay alive, they can hammer our financial returns. Most large firms look at them and decide they aren't worth acquiring at any price. So, on down the beach they go, eating our money without any real prospect of returning it.

Unlike the individual from my company, these are tough to handle. Sometimes, however, we have found ways to lessen the pain. One is simply to stop funding them. We don't walk away; we're still there to help with ideas and guidance. But we don't feed them either. Those Grunts sometimes find techniques to get on a cash diet and survive. Once in a very great while they find themselves a home (via an M&A event) and give back at least a fraction of the money we invested. But usually they die of starvation. RIP. If you find a crab in your organization, I suggest you consider a crab feed. Kill it yourself and redeploy the good people there where they can contribute to the growth of your company.

In chapter eleven you'll read about a human resources organization that receives a Grunt rating during the conclusion of Chris Jameson's adventure. That is not a slam on HR groups, as I've seen many that operate with very high marks across the board. However, there was one time when I saw an HR group move from Success stature to Grunt in a remarkably short period.

In this case, the driver of the change was much like my colleague who saw his job rise above his ability to handle complexity. The company in question initially had created the HR group to do two things: to help recruit high caliber engineers at our home office, and to make sure the company was complying with all laws and regulations. They did a terrific job at both. However, as the company grew, new requirements arose. We needed people in *all* functional areas. We needed people at *all* management levels. We needed people in *all geographies*, including internationally.

At first we just handed these additional requirements to the original HR group. But in short order we discovered they had devolved from Success mode to Grunt status. They were still finding and helping hire some key people, but we could see them becoming increasingly frazzled as they did so. And that led to some important hiring mistakes and almost serious legal trouble in one international setting, where the employment rules were very different.

Once we realized the problem, we ratcheted back expectations for the group to what they originally had been. The US sales organization was given the charter to source its own talent, coordinating with corporate HR when making offers. Our international operations were given full HR responsibilities for their major geographies, with country managers coordinating with a HR person in their region. We turned the Grunt back into a Success, and helped create some additional Successes across the enterprise. That model of "outsourcing," either within or beyond your organization's walls, can work wonders with well-meaning Grunts.

THREE EASY STEPS TO IDENTIFY A GRUNT

- Ask, "What are you doing differently today from a year ago?" If the answer is "Nothing," you probably have a Grunt. If they actually *say* nothing, you may have another sort of problem. Grunts do not tend to be even the least bit introspective. If they were, they might consider a Vision worth having or a Process worth employing, and no longer be a Grunt. If they can talk about how their Process has changed or is changing, then maybe you have a Merchant, not a Grunt.

- Check their pulse rate. If the circumstances surrounding this person or organization have changed in some material way, check to see if they are running harder just to stay in place. Grunts who are expected to improve their

Output as the treadmill speeds up may survive for a bit. But before long they will become exhausted, stop running, and the treadmill will send them careening.

- Ask for Vision. Grunts and Brutes often can be confused for each other. But Brutes can articulate their Vision, even if they don't have a sustainable Process to achieve it. Ask, "What do you think you'll need to do differently a year from now to achieve (y)our Vision?" A Grunt won't even understand the question. Speaking of questions, I generally hate the standard interviewer ploy, "Where do you see yourself in X years?" But here's a case where it can be quite useful. If the person or organization can't answer that with any clarity, then you've found a Grunt.

YOU'VE FOUND A GRUNT, NOW WHAT?

A Grunt can be a terrific resource, or a group that is close to becoming a Loser. Your job is to figure out which you have, and act accordingly.

- Reduce their complexity or scope of responsibility. As you saw with both the individual and the HR organization in this chapter, the issue was their inability to deal with complexity. This is not a value statement, just a fact. If you can get the person or group to ignore their ego and focus on what's good for the enterprise, they can be managed successfully and moved into a more appropriate position.

- Introduce some defined Processes. Getting a Grunt all the way to Success mode can be hard. But if you can get them to Merchant status, you are on the right track. If you can find some simple Processes for them that actually make their world easier to understand and operate in, then you've made progress. However, be advised that a Grunt already over their complexity limit may see new Process as added complexity and implode into Loser status. Not a pretty sight.

- Team them with others, but with clear limits on role and expectations. Going back to the quotation at the beginning of this chapter, Grunts can be the last thing between you and the wolf at the door. And many will lay their life on the line (at least in an organizational sense) to fight off that wolf. So team them with others who can appreciate their Output, and who can provide the Vision and Process you need to win. In the military, there is a reason the chain of command works (most of the time). The generals have the overall plan for the war (the Vision). The captains and lieutenants develop plans to gain territory (the Process). And the sergeants and privates storm the hill. The war isn't won by generals, although they can lose it. (See D-Day reaction by the Nazi high command.) The war is won by the Grunts, but only when they have someone providing proper Vision and Process so they end up with a Success-ful campaign.

YOUR PERSONAL GRUNT

Are you a Grunt in your personal life? Do you not see yourself in some different role in five or ten years? Do you have no goals, and no plans to create or achieve any? Maybe you are caught in an "activity trap." An activity trap snaps shut when you are so consumed with the day to day that *all you can see* is that day to day existence.

We all get stymied in this trap, more often than we'd like to admit. We are on the treadmill of life, with jobs and families and other events all clamoring for our time, attention and energy. So we keep running just to stay in place.

There once was a well-known hair coloring ad that claimed, "You're not getting older, you're getting better!" Alas, it's more likely that most of us are just getting older. Getting better requires a Vision of what "getting better" means, and a Process to achieve that.

Ask yourself what you might do differently to have the energy to consider a longer term plan. Sometimes, when you do this, you'll find some of those running in place tasks can be delegated to others, or simply dropped from your list. Like the consultant who raised the "Why not take the risk to call high?" in the Personal Academic section in chapter four, ask yourself what would happen if you didn't do a certain thing as much, or at all.

As a trivial example, take the issue of making your bed every morning. Many of us have figured out that this is a completely Grunt (and worthless) exercise. Why make it if you are only going to unmake it the next evening? Unless you are showing off your bedroom (how often does that happen?), who cares if the sheets and blankets are smooth and tidy? We all "make our beds" in ways that use our energies poorly, when they could be better spent on a Vision for the future and in taking even small Process steps to achieve those goals.

NINE

The Loser

"Show me a good loser, and I'll show you a loser."
Vince Lombardi

It would be easy to make this a one-paragraph chapter. However, Losers have a real place in business and in life. No, not as road kill. Losers are often the character or group most willing to accept needed change. If you have no Vision, no Process and no Output, you will listen to anyone who can help you. Organizations so calcified that they resist attempts to improve them usually start listening about the time everyone starts writing their obituary.

In chapter eight, you read how added complexity can turn a Success into a Grunt. Even worse, too much complexity can turn a Success into a Loser. In one of my first venture capital investments, I experienced this firsthand. I was attending a board meeting of one of our startups when the CEO excused himself because he was feeling ill. The VPs continued to present their functional areas, but there was notable tension in the room that I didn't understand.

Finally, the most experienced of the VPs told the board that all of them felt the CEO was not able to lead them anymore. In fact, it was so bad they issued an ultimatum: "Either he goes or we go!" Needless to say, we were shocked. We knew the company was having problems, but not that it had gotten to this level.

We did some additional discovery and came to understand that, as the company had grown, and things had become more complex, the CEO essentially had frozen at the controls. He would not make any key decisions for fear of being wrong. But also he wouldn't let the VPs make any key decisions. So when it came to choosing whether to fire the CEO, fire the VPs, or try to get everyone to play nicely together, we went with the first option.

To his credit, the CEO took his dismissal professionally. Frankly, I think he was relieved, because he must have been terribly stressed that he was in that far over his head. Once we turned the VPs loose to make decisions while we searched for a new CEO, the company started performing again. Many Losers are simply well-meaning, hardworking people who are in over their heads. Sometimes organizations that have become Losers just need new leadership. The important thing is, when you find a Loser, treat it as a fire, not just a fire drill.

This happened to me at Mentor Graphics. After years of unparalleled success, we fell victim to Vision creep, followed by process bloating, followed by product development slippage. The result was that suddenly we were staring at two consecutive years of $50M losses. Fortunately, we had more than $100M in cash, and we had very loyal (or, some might say, very locked-in) customers. We got the chance to come to our senses (finally) and painfully restart the engine that had stalled. Had we continued to have even mediocre results, we might not have recovered in time. It was the sudden severity of the decline that saved us.

Mentor Graphics descended to Loser status by combining complexity and complacency. Once we beat our primary early competitor, Daisy Systems, we embarked on increasingly grand Visions (see: *The Vision Trap*). That was because we "had won" (note: you have never truly "won:" you have to do it every day) and held the misguided belief that the market position we had achieved was readily defensible. Mix in the arrogance that comes from winning, and thinking that we could now win at everything we tried, and we added tremendous complexity in the form of new business ventures and, later, a new generation of software.

Our odyssey to an ambitious but blurred Vision led to Processes that were not the substantial, proven ones that fueled our early Success, which led to delayed Output that was not customer-focused. Fortunately, the fall was sudden and hard enough, and our cash reserves were large enough, that we were able to wake up (think cold water in the face), get back to basics (over time) and return to serving our customers. We lost our market leadership position, but we didn't lose the enterprise. Today, Mentor Graphics has over $1 billion in revenue, so the story continues. But complacency and complexity almost ended it.

Sometimes, it's neither complacency nor complexity that takes a Success and creates a Loser. It's a clever competitor. When I worked at Tektronix the company had a fledgling business unit called MEG: Mechanical Engineering Graphics. That group produced systems used by mechanical engineers to design three dimensional objects ranging from computer enclosures to jet aircraft. The leading company in the computer-aided design (CAD) field at that time was Computervision, located outside of Boston. But Tektronix, while late to the market, had a distinct advantage. Then, before the high resolution "raster" displays we all take for granted in our computer monitors and TV sets today, the only way to display the high quality graphics needed for mechanical design was to use a "direct view storage tube," or DVST. (If you are curious about what those looked like, watch a rerun of the original Battlestar Galactica TV show and the fighter cockpit displays.) As it turned out, Tektronix held the patent on the DVST, and, while it sold them at a handsome profit to all the CAD companies, including Computervision, Tek would have an enormous cost advantage if they built their own systems.

Surprisingly, while customers were enthused that Tektronix could offer these systems at a substantially lower price than Computervision (due to the DVST cost advantage) sales were slow to ramp up. Finally Tektronix management, tired of losing money in the startup stage of the business, pulled the plug on MEG. It never had the aura of a Success inside the company, and was permanently relegated to the Loser's scrap heap. But here's where the tale gets interesting …

When we were starting Mentor Graphics a few years later, we visited with the former CEO of Computervision to see if he could give us some advice, since we were not going to be a competitor in their CAD domain. And he told us *the other side of the story.*

Tek's MEG was indeed winning, just before it was shut

down. Computervision was running scared because Tektronix, with its better cost position, reputation for high quality products and extensive global sales presence, could seize market share. But Computervision noticed that, while Tek had a number of product lines in test and measurement instrumentation and in the graphic display business, two of those—oscilloscopes and DVSTs—held share positions in the 80% level in their respective markets, with correspondingly huge profits.

Computervision assumed (correctly) that Tek wasn't used to being in a bar fight. Tek was so accustomed to commanding market positions, and the comfort they provided, that they would run from a brawl. So Computervision executives held hands with wavering customers, offered price cuts if needed, and sold "futures" about the next great technology they planned to introduce. Essentially, they would do or say whatever they needed to slow Tektronix down.

They started a fight.

And it worked: Tektronix got a bloody nose, and fled.

Losers come in many guises. If you can figure out how they got there, you have a much better chance of turning them around.

THREE EASY STEPS TO IDENTIFY A LOSER

- Work backwards. Start with Output, which is the easiest to measure. You can probably tell right away if it's missing. Moving further upstream to understand whether Process and Vision are lacking can be more difficult. Many a Dreamer or Academic has been labeled a Loser by those not willing to look deeper. Or, as you'll see in the next chapter, lack of Output simply can be Successes just about to show themselves: if their Vision and Process are solid.

- Check for talent drain. Again, with a preview of chapter ten, employees vote with their feet. If you have an organization that is, or is about to be, a Loser, one of the key things you'll notice is talent walking out the door. Great people have options. And no one likes to go down with the ship, especially if they've been trying to tell the captain for some time to steer clear of that iceberg ahead. We see this in startups all the time. Those who are on the road to trouble start to see people defecting, even before we see all the problems clearly. Many times, exit interviews will not give you the full story because departing employees don't want to cast stones at their colleagues. But if you see a rush to the exits, beware of a Loser in your midst.

- Test for fatalism. There comes a point when those in an organization or, for that matter, an individual, can simply give up and say to themselves (and you), "Well, I guess we're screwed." And at that point the chances you *are* screwed are nearly 100%. If the team has given up the fight, you might as well end the game, because the score will not improve.

Remarkably, some people can reach the point of conceding defeat, but keep marching on together, burning cash and burning out their souls. The good ones have already left. But the rest may throw in the towel, yet hang around nonetheless. If you see this fatalistic resignation in your midst, you know you have a Loser.

YOU'VE FOUND A LOSER, NOW WHAT?

As strange as it sounds, Losers can be tough, but also can be one of the easiest groups to deal with.

- Offer assistance. Smart Losers, and there are many of them, are the most receptive to new ideas and new direction. In fact, they are desperate for any semblance of leadership that can give them hope. Sadly, this is why you see so many lost souls attached to the cult du jour. They see in that cult leader a chance to feel good about themselves and have a sense of belonging. But you don't need to be a cultist to take advantage of a Loser's predicament. A good, well-intentioned leader will do just fine. Losers who have found new hope can be turned into valuable members of the team … in time.
- Get back to basics. If a Loser has been overwhelmed from too much complexity, put

them back on a "walk before you run" path. Giving Losers simple goals and Processes, with clear and relatively immediate Output requirements, can rebuild their confidence and let them get ready to stretch their wings again. In fact, I saw this first hand during the dark days at Mentor Graphics. Once we got back to basics, people began to take pride in doing the fundamentals well. And that pride and dedication led to the company's revival.

- Replace or Outsource. Of course, not every Loser can be turned into a winner. Sometimes that person or that organization really is the "weakest link," and the best course of action is to say goodbye. It may be that the easiest way to handle that is to take what had been an internal function and outsource it. That has the advantage of immediate relief and also sends a warning shot across the bow of other groups: "Either perform or we'll get someone who can." The same is true for individual contributors. I can't tell you how many times I've agonized over removing an employee, feeling that others would view it negatively, only to be asked by the rank and file, "What took you so long? That idiot has been a drag on us for years. Just having him gone will improve our productivity, even before you replace him with a good person!"

YOUR PERSONAL LOSER

Are you a Loser in your personal life? Actually, if you've read this far, there is a very low probability you are. You've at least taken one concrete step towards thinking about the Vision, Process and Output of your life. But still you may have doubts. If so, here's what to do:

- Get back to basics yourself. Take an inventory of what has happened in your life that makes you wonder if you've slipped into Loser status. What seems to be wrong? What can you change? How would that make a difference? Creating a simple set of life goals, and a set of activities you might undertake to reach them, and what visible milestones you might monitor to measure your progress, is a place to start.

- Set a new direction for yourself. To restart your Vision, you may need visionaries. Take a class, join a new organization, or make a new friend. Find a new purpose. Not many of us can fix all our problems on our own. If we find ourselves losing and lost, a helping hand would be nice. But the strongest helping hand is your own. Join a service organization you've always admired, or a company you've always wanted to work for. Most important, look for people or organizations that have what you are lacking. Let them show you the way.

- Start with baby steps, or giant leaps. Usually it works best if you take some small steps in a new direction, because that feels less risky, and often offers the easier path to initial, reinforcing success. But sometimes a shock to the system is needed. Just as a company faces impending bankruptcy and suddenly gets religion on cost control and cash management, perhaps you need to take a look at yourself and leap, rather than gently step, into a new you. We see this all the time with people suddenly recovering from what they thought were terminal illnesses, or those who manage to cheat death in some accident. Don't wait for terrifying circumstances to become the person you always wanted to be.

- Start now. What have you got to lose?

TEN

The Success

"Success is a lousy teacher. It seduces smart people into thinking they can't lose."

Bill Gates

OK, you've made it. You have a solid, sensible Vision. Your Processes are in place and working well. Products are rolling out to eager customers. Profits are pouring in. "What, me worry?" (Thank you, Alfred E. Newman). Actually, yes. But first, pat yourself on the back. While The Success Matrix is easy to understand, it is not easy to implement. If you have done so, you are among the highest performing individuals or firms on the planet. But don't let your guard down for a second. Once you are cashing those fat bonus checks, it gets very tempting to focus only on Output (which is where 95% of bonus checks come from), and forget about the role Vision and Process played in getting you to the promised land. And, left unattended, Vision erodes first, then Process, and before long Output is under fire. By then, it is too late to recover without serious, painful consequences.

The good news is that some very successful companies have modeled not only the way to get to Success, but also the way to stay there. In fact, in my venture capital firm we have firsthand experience (sort of) with two that you will recognize right way: Amazon and Starbucks. I say "sort of," because we also have real pain associated with both firms. In the late 1980s, Howard Schultz of Starbucks approached our firm (before my time, I'm pleased to report) and presented his business plan. My future partners listened to the pitch politely and, after he left the room, shared a "knowing" response: "Who in their right mind would pay $2.00 (late 1980s, remember) for a cup of coffee you can get for less than 50 cents?" And so our firm turned down arguably one of the most successful startups of all time.

In the case of Amazon, the situation was different. In 1994, when Internet retailing was completely unproven, Amazon had just $4 million in sales. We had a handshake agreement with them to invest $2 million for a 20% stake in the company (a $10 million implied company value). But before we could consummate the transaction, a well-known Silicon Valley venture capitalist offered $8 million for 20% (a $40 million company value). Of course, Amazon went with the $8 million deal, and as a result neither I nor my partners are traveling today in our private jets.

The travails of our venture firm notwithstanding, we can say we saw both deals in their formative stage with their initial business plans. And so we can comment on the evolution of those firms over time, regardless of what folklore may have grown up about how grand their Vision was when they started.

When Starbucks came to us looking for investment dollars, they had a solid Vision of creating a community gathering place, based on European cafes. This essentially was a model of the neighborhood tavern, with caffeine replacing alcohol. Initially, the focus was exclusively on coffee and a sense of place. The special drinks created the draw, while the "comfort" of each store was designed to encourage customers not just to buy coffee and leave, but instead to linger. And, as we've all witnessed over time, the real estate department at Starbucks was viewed as a core strategic asset, getting the rights to high traffic, high visibility locations at first, and then filling in around them.

Over time, however, Starbucks realized that to continue to grow same store sales, they needed to offer more products to get a larger "share of wallet" from their customers. With that came products from food to music to coffee making equipment. Now, the latter surprised me at first. They were essentially encouraging people to make their own Starbucks at home. That couldn't possibly be as profitable as selling in the store. Right?

Wrong. What I didn't understand was that the Starbucks "brand" was transcending the Starbucks "place." As their Vision has evolved over time, Starbucks has added to its Process by selling products with their brand name in other locations, such as grocery stores. As of this writing, they are about to add a co-branded line of yogurt. Of course, not every new product has worked out for them. But Starbucks has been relentless, not just in expanding geographically (look out, Asia!) but by systematically adjusting their Vision and layering in Process to increase same store sales, and even to eclipse the concept of a "store" as a limit to their growth. That has kept Output growing and their shareholders happy. Now, if my partners had only been smart enough to invest in the early days …

If Starbucks has done a good job carefully growing what the franchise and brand represent, Amazon has raised the bar even higher. When they showed us their original business plan, it was only for books. Period. While now there are some who say the "original plan" was always more grand, we have data to disprove that. But that makes what they did even more impressive.

Sure, once they figured out how to sell books via the Internet, and figured out how a recommendation engine ("If you bought this, you'll probably like this") could increase revenues, the move to selling other items was logical. While the breadth of product they now offer is astonishing, they moved that way carefully and successfully after establishing solid footing in books, with essentially the same Vision and Process they had for books.

But this is where they moved to another dimension. It is one thing to develop a software platform to run your business. It is quite another to open up that platform and embrace a wide range of sellers to comprise a virtual storefront. It's why I said for many years that Amazon wasn't really a retailer; instead, they were a database company disguised as a retailer. They simply took the Vision and Processes they perfected for internal use and turned them loose. But even then, my understanding of their business was too limited.

Another asset Amazon owned was tens of thousands of Linux servers to run the company, because they had to have massive computing capacity to handle the December holiday rush, even if much of that would sit idle the remainder of the year. So they looked at that asset and asked, "Why don't we make that available to others?" And Amazon Web Services was born, offering dramatically lower cost computing resources to other firms, since anything they were paid for those idle assets was essentially free gross margin. Again, they took part of their Vision (our network can never go down, because we lose sales if we are offline for even a minute), and their Process (we have to have virtually unlimited computing capacity to handle peak demand) and leveraged their internal Output to the outside world.

Our venture firm once held a technology conference to which we invited luminaries from the computing industry, and one of the sessions was on Internet security. Amazon's CTO (who was on our advisory committee) attended, and the talk turned to what large companies could do about DNS (denial of service) attacks from computer hackers. I turned to the Amazon CTO and said, "If I had tens of thousands of Linux servers under my control and was hit with a DNS attack, I'd be tempted to launch a counter attack." He replied with a twinkle in his eye, "Who's to say we don't?"

It was ironic to learn some years later that in the Edward Snowden affair Amazon was implicated in the NSA snooping issue. But you can understand that, as their Vision morphed from being a database company with an Internet retail front-end to being a computing resources company, all that power could be used for many purposes. In any event, Amazon is a prime example of how a Success in one domain can find a way, over time, to move into areas where they have expertise or available assets, without falling victim to complacency or adding unmanageable complexity.

Shifting from a corporate to an individual example, I can recall a rather awkward time for me with one of the first sales representatives for Mentor Graphics. I had gotten to know Scott when we both worked at Tektronix, and he was consistently among the top sales people in the company. So when we were staffing Mentor, I was delighted when he decided to join us, covering his home territory of southern California.

But then, nothing happened. Scott came on board near the beginning of the calendar year; yet, by October, he had not closed a single order. I was very concerned that he was going to quit, since he wasn't making the large commissions he had earned at Tektronix. I flew down to spend a day on customer calls with Scott, hoping to encourage him. He met me at the John Wayne airport in Orange County, and off we went to see some of the largest electronics companies in the region.

While we knew each other well, there clearly was tension. I assumed that was the result of my concern that he might be planning to leave Mentor. I'll come back in a moment to what I saw during my visit. But to cut to the chase, as he drove me back to the airport at the end of the day he turned to me and blurted out, "Well, if you're going to fire me, would you just get it over with?" While I was worrying about Scott quitting, he was well aware that he hadn't closed any business in eight months, and assumed I had come down as a courtesy, rather than firing him over the phone. Needless to say, his question broke the ice, and we had a good laugh and a constructive talk while I waited for my flight. But here's what I saw that convinced me he hadn't lost his sales mojo.

In meeting after meeting, Scott had a clear vision of the value our products offered these large customers, and he explained that value very clearly, handling the occasional objection with professionalism and class. He also understood and navigated the politics of each customer, in that our systems threatened the traditional power structure of the CAD (computer aided design) department by putting our new tools directly on the engineers' desks. He also knew who was an economic buyer, where ROI mattered, and who was a technical buyer, where the specifications were paramount. In other words, his Vision and his Process were spot on.

Scott was not an Academic; he was a Success being judged too soon. The Mentor Graphics systems at that time cost over $100,000 each, and most engineering organizations purchased more than one. From a corporate budget perspective, this was usually a quarter million dollar decision, or more. Not only were those decisions not made quickly, they also usually had to have budget assigned to them as part of an annual planning process.

But Scott had come on board in February, well after most customer budgets were in place for the calendar year. And so, while he could sell as effectively as ever, the customers were holding off, working internally for capital budget dollars for the following year. And the proof of this?

Scott did close a few small orders after my October visit. Nonetheless, he probably had his lowest income in many years. But he didn't quit, and he certainly wasn't fired. The following year, against a $2 million quota, he sold over $7 million worth of equipment and was the highest paid person in the company, including me and other top management. Even in subsequent years, when we raised his quota, he always found a way to beat his objectives for the year and show up, smiling, at the annual Sales Achievement Club event.

What we had in Scott was a budding Success who just needed a little more time to bloom. The lesson: always evaluate the Vision and Process to decide whether that is all there is, or if you just have to wait a bit to see the Output flow!

THREE EASY STEPS TO IDENTIFY A SUCCESS

- The success they are having appears almost effortless. We've all seen professional athletes perform in ways we mere mortals can only dream about. And they perform with such apparent ease that it belies all the hard work that went into making it look so simple. A Success can make you think that whatever they are doing must not really be that hard, but don't be fooled. If you see Output flowing with a grace that you know, deep down, doesn't reflect the challenge of the task, then you probably have a Success on your hands. Lucky you!

- High quality talent is flowing to them. As noted in chapter nine about the Loser, people vote with their feet—both coming and going.

If you see an organization that suddenly seems able to attract the best and the brightest, those folks have probably figured out, before you have, that they can be part of a Success. Whatever sixth sense people have about joining a winning team, it's real. When we look at some of the startups we have backed, the real Successes rarely mention how hard it is for them to find talent, while those who are not real Successes often do. If you see people rushing to get on board, you should too.

- They start thinking bigger. As with Starbucks and Amazon, this can be a good thing. But as with Mentor Graphics and others, it can also be a bad thing. Like the mythological Sirens, grand Visions can kill, especially if they lead the organization beyond the limits of its skills and talent. Yet incremental additions to the Vision, if managed well and executed nearly flawlessly, can sustain an enterprise for years.

YOU'VE FOUND A SUCCESS, NOW WHAT?

Success is a precious and fragile commodity. Getting there is hard, but staying there can be even harder. Human nature is a powerful force, and the tendency to either ease up and revel in the moment, or try to leap too far ahead, is part of our business DNA. But here's what you can do to avoid both problems.

- Ride them hard. Add responsibility, but carefully. Riding them hard helps avoid complacency, but also risks adding too much complexity. And holding the hill is as hard as taking it. I learned this years ago when, after my company had some success, we found ourselves caught between trying to do what our existing customers wanted us to do to support and enhance our products, and what new customers were demanding. It turned out their "care-abouts" were somewhat different, while our engineering resources were finite. And in our sales team, we ultimately had to differentiate between "explorers," who had the mindset to go after new accounts, and "farmers," who would better serve existing accounts and look for ways to get them to expand their business over time.

- Set them up as role models. While Mark Twain famously said, "There is nothing so annoying as a good example," it is also true that a good example can motivate others to follow the leader. Both organizations and individuals who exhibit all the attributes of a Success can be powerful forces for progress, as long as when you use them you point to all three attributes of their success not just their Output. Take the time to discover and understand the aspects of Vision and Process you believe others in the enterprise need to emulate, and make those the examples you share.

- Keep checking upstream. No matter how hard you try, it is natural for Successes to start to focus more on Output, where they see immediate rewards, than on the longer term issues of Vision and Process. Beware, for success can be fleeting. And the garden needs constant weeding.

YOUR PERSONAL SUCCESS

Are you a Success in your personal life? Do you have everything in balance and are you seeing your vision realized, your Process honed and your personal Output achieved? Well, why in the world have you taken the time to read this far? Perhaps it's because at some level you appreciate how perishable Success is and how you need always to be on guard to keep it fresh.

- Stay focused. If you have become successful, it may be that what got you there won't necessarily keep you there, but it's a good place to start. And remember, as with MJ in chapter one, being a personal Success doesn't have to involve some grandiose activity. I know a woman who is a gourmet chef. She really enjoys cooking not only terrific tasting but terrific looking meals for her family and friends. Her Vision to do that is coupled with an ongoing Process to devour (sorry) all the

major cooking magazines and newspaper
articles she can get her hands on, and to take
not only the recipes but the photos of the
prepared dishes to heart. Of course, as an
experienced chef she modifies many of the
recipes slightly to her own taste and creative
nature. But, she has found a Success model,
and in that area of her life she can repeat the
model over and over.

- Stay grounded. The fact you are a Success
  in one area does not guarantee you will be a
  Success in others. While in chapter one Henry
  talked about how MJ was a Success in multiple
  ways, he did that organically, without lofty or
  unrealistic expectations. As you step from an
  area in life where you feel competent into one
  where you are not as comfortable, give yourself
  permission to try and fail, or marginally
  succeed; then learn, and go again.

- Stay balanced. Just like organizations, we all
  get attracted to Output. So if you are a Success
  who has melded Vision and Process well into
  your life, along with Output, pat yourself on
  the back. But then take some time to reflect on
  whether you still are as energized about your
  Vision and still as committed to your Process
  as you once were. If you are not, those will
  atrophy, and someday you'll be focused at the
  end of a different chapter in this book.

With that, let's get back to Chris Jameson and see how

he's doing with that big meeting in New York.

ELEVEN

The Success Matrix at Work

The thump of the plane's tires touching down at La-Guardia jarred Chris from his slumber. The flight took less than an hour, but he felt remarkably refreshed. He took a cab to the hotel, settled in and began to think hard about how to handle his morning assignment.

His plan came to him gradually. He'd have to engage his audience in a way that initially was non-threatening, so he'd need to hold off on the character names for a while. Also he didn't want to explain the entire Success Matrix right away. He would have neither the time nor, early in the meeting, the trust of his potential direct reports. He needed to get them to reveal themselves and their position in the Success Matrix in a way that could be synthesized, on the fly, into something they all could talk about. Finally, he recognized there was a real risk in taking this approach. What if they decided to undermine the process and give him bogus information? What if his little experiment blew up in his face in front of the CEO selection committee?

Well, he wasn't going to get his dream job by being conservative. They were looking for a hard charger, so he would charge!

Chris once had worked in a marketing organization where an application called SurveyMonkey was used to poll customers. It had a number of useful features that could be used to his advantage with the group tomorrow. He opened his laptop, accessed the application, and began to construct a survey to administer to the Ultramax VPs.

He was a bit out of practice with the application, and worked on it until 2 AM. Not too bad for someone still on West Coast time, but he needed to be up at 7 AM East Coast to get ready. Nonetheless, when he was finished he felt better about how this approach was going to work out. Maybe he'd really learn something about this organization using the Success Matrix approach. Even better, maybe THEY might learn something. That would be the big win. If the search committee saw him leading the company to better understand itself in several *hours*, they might just let him lead that company for several *years*. Sleep was elusive as he continued to think about how the morning might play out.

At 8:30 AM, 30 minutes before his meeting, he walked into the Ultramax lobby. He was escorted into the large conference room with the ominous mirror along one wall. As he had requested, there was a projector in the center of the table and flip charts and markers in one corner. He wrote the definitions of the three components of the Matrix on one of the charts—one on each page. He then stuck those three pages on the wall, covering each with another sheet from the pad so no one would see them until he was ready. Then he wrote the eight possible outcomes of the Matrix, but left off the character names for the time being. Finally he connected his laptop to the projector and made sure everything worked. So far, so good.

He took some coffee from the side table and waited.

A few minutes later the headhunter walked in with the board chair. They all shook hands and chatted briefly before reviewing the day's agenda. As they were talking, his potential direct reports began to file in. They eyed him carefully, like elephants watching an approaching lion. Fight or flight? Chris felt his neck tighten and his face flush just a bit. He drank more coffee to keep his mouth from getting any drier.

"Get a grip," he said to himself. "I'm going to be the one in charge here, better start acting like it!"

Everyone settled into their chairs, the headhunter and board chair left for the one-way mirror room, and Chris cleared his throat.

"Thank you all for coming, not that you had a lot of choice." This was greeted with some strained smiles. "I'm Chris Jameson, and as you know I'm one of the finalists for the CEO position. What I'd like to do is have each of you introduce yourselves and explain what part of the company you are responsible for. After we get aquainted, I have a process I'd like us to go through to help me understand the strengths and weakness of Ultramax, and how we might make it even better than it is."

As soon as those last words left his lips he thought, "Damn, that sounded gratuitous. I'll bet the folks behind the glass all gagged."

The people were starting to introduce themselves, so he refocused on them. Given the nature of the company, the VPs managed the expected functional areas: R&D, marketing, sales, manufacturing, finance and human resources. After they all had spoken, Chris spent a few minutes describing his own background, and then redirected the conversation.

"Great. Now we all know each other a little bit better. I have each of your email addresses, and I'm going to use them for the next stage of our conversation. I'd like you all to take out your smart phones or tablets and look for an email from me. I'll hit send now, so you should have it in a few moments." He paused. "When you open the email, you'll find a very simple survey that I hope will stimulate and inform our interaction over the rest of the day." Chris got up and walked to the three covered flip chart pages. "To me, all the key aspects of a business can be broken down into three basic elements: Vision, Process and Output. That may sound simplistic, but bear with me for a bit."

He removed the cover sheets. As a reminder, here's what he had written.

VISION

"A broadly understood sense of direction which encompasses competitive leadership over time."

PROCESS

"The structures, methods and procedures to repeatedly produce timely, high quality products or services, independent of changes in personnel."

OUTPUT

"Profitable products and services are being produced with predictable regularity."

Chris then reviewed each definition, much as Henry had done with him, but with an added twist. "Now, I know that these are fairly high level, and they may not apply exactly for each organization within Ultramax. But I believe that for each of your functional groups there is at least some slightly modified version of these that would. Please take some time to think about how you'd apply this framework to the organization you manage."

Chris could see from the body language that not everyone was buying in to his model. That was no surprise. He'd felt the same way in Vermont after almost a day at this exercise. These people had seen it for less than ten minutes.

"OK," Chris said. "Now I'd like you to open the survey I sent you. You'll find each is personalized, so that the organization you manage is at the top, with those of your colleagues below. What I'd like you to do now is rate your department, as well as those of your peers here, on a scale of 1 to 10 on those three dimensions. Ten means you are absolutely nailing the category. A one means it's missing in action. Don't worry about precision; I'm not looking for perfection. When you're done, hit 'finish' at the end of the survey and it will come back to me."

Chris stood up and walked to the side table, refilling his coffee. It was show time. This was either going to work or he was going to look like a fool.

After what seemed an eternity, but was closer five minutes, he saw on his laptop that all the surveys had come back in. He encouraged everyone to take a break and get something to drink while he looked over the data. He was pleased, and relieved, by what he saw. "Let's get back to it," he said. "First, let's see how each of you rated your own organization."

Chris had arranged a set of tabs so he could quickly toggle through various views of the data. He chose the one labeled "Self-score" and popped it to the top. At the same time, that page was projected on the wall.

Self-score

Organization	Vision	Process	Output
Marketing	9	8	9
Sales	9	9	10
R&D	8	9	9
Finance	9	9	9
Manufacturing	9	9	8
Human Resources	9	9	9

"Well, will you look at that?" Chris exclaimed. "You all rated yourselves as excellent across all three dimensions! A few eights, mostly nines, with one brave soul (oh, that's Sales, what a shock) with a ten for their Output. I guess my work here is done. You don't need a CEO after all."

Finally he got a few real laughs rather than tense smiles.

"But before I leave, perhaps it would be worthwhile to see how you rated each other. I doubt it's much different, but you never know." Chris was trying his best to keep a straight face. "Before we look at the numbers, there are two things you should know that I'm going to do here over the next few minutes. First, because we are going to start by looking at the averages of your scores, I need to normalize for those who are easy graders and those who are stingier. I can always go back and show you the raw results if you like. But, by sliding each of your scores around slightly so the mid-points of your ranges coincide, it makes for a better comparison." Chris picked another survey, "Other's Score." The numbers flashed up on the wall, and the room got very quiet.

Other's Average Score (normalized)

Organization	Vision	Process	Output
Marketing	6.2	5.1	5.9
Sales	4.9	5.9	6.8
R&D	7.5	5.3	3.9
Finance	5.0	7.7	4.7
Manufacturing	5.4	7.2	6.1
Human Resources	4.4	5.1	6.5

"Now, isn't that interesting." Chris feigned surprise. "All those eights and nines are gone. Now we see averages from the mid sevens all the way down to the high threes. It seems that while each of you grade yourself very highly, your fellow VPs here aren't so generous. It reminds me of one of those pop psychology books from years ago titled, 'I'm OK! You're OK!' Except you've just changed it to, 'I'm OK! You ... not so much!'"

That got a few wan smiles in the room, but that was all. This was serious and everyone knew they were being observed through the mirror.

"Now, for the second part of the data adjustment, let's take this analog representation of your collective judgment and make it starker and more digital. What I'm going to do is use this slider at the bottom of the screen to have the system collect the results into two categories, either above or below the cut-off. Looking at what we have, let's pick something in the low fives, like 5.2, and see what happens."

The screen changed from numeric to the same sort of table Henry Long had sketched for Chris less than two days earlier. And the result was dramatic:

Other's Average Score (binary)

Organization	Vision	Process	Output
Marketing	X	–	X
Sales	–	X	X
R&D	X	X	–
Finance	–	X	–
Manufacturing	X	X	X
Human Resources	–	–	X

Chris continued, "You'll note that R&D has an X for Vision and Process, but not Output. And if I move the slider just a bit higher on the cut-off scale, to 5.4, the Process attribute also goes away. On the other hand, Finance has a rock solid position with Process, but is missing both Vision and Output. Sales has no Vision, but has Process and Output. HR, you're light on Vision and Process. Manufacturing, apparently you can take the rest of the day off (although you just barely make it on Vision)! Now, let me add one more thing to our table. First, I'll go to the final flip chart I had covered up. You'll see those conditions all shown here, the eight possible situations with the presence or absence of the attributes of Vision, Process and Output. I have some shorthand labels I use for each, and I'll add them now."

Chris filled in the character names: Dreamer, Academic, Brute, Bureaucrat, Merchant, Grunt, Loser and Success. The room went absolutely still. Back at his laptop, Chris chose one other tab that added the character names to each functional department's score.

Other's Average Score (character)

Organization	Vision	Process	Output
Marketing - Brute	X	–	X
Sales - Merchant	–	X	X
R&D - Academic	X	X	–
Finance - Bureaucrat	–	X	–
Manufacturing - Success	X	X	X
Human Resources - Grunt	–	–	X

"Don't be alarmed," Chris said. "This isn't a witch hunt. This is just a vehicle to find out where each of us might need to improve and, more importantly, if the organization is operating in balance. Every part of the company doesn't have to be in Success mode (not that there is anything wrong with that!). But working together, collectively we must be a Success. One organization's strengths have to cover another's weaknesses, while we all try to improve. This 'Success Matrix' is designed to give us a common

framework and a common vocabulary to identify our issues and then address them. Let me go back to the survey
data and show you what I mean. Let's take Marketing. By
the luck of the draw, you're first on the list." The Marketing
VP did not look pleased.

Chris selected another tab. "If we look behind the averages, you can see that while the team on average rates
you as a Brute, Sales rates you as an Academic (Vision and
Process, but no Output). But R&D sees you as a Merchant
(no Vision, but Process and Output). Maybe Sales is saying
you need to do a better job with the Output they need, such
as qualified sales leads, while R&D is complaining that you
are too reactive to the competitive feature du jour and not
thinking about long term product superiority. I don't know
if those characterizations are fair, but I've seen enough in
my past experience to think they might be.

"Now, let's look at Sales. The overall group ranked you
as a Merchant, but Finance tags you as a Grunt, saying that
while you have Output, you really don't have a sustainable
Process. Perhaps that CRM (customer relationship management) system you have is not being used properly, and
Finance is hanging on by their fingernails at the end of the
quarter, not knowing if you're going to make or miss the
revenue and earnings expectations Wall Street has for you.

"You all have labeled Finance as a Bureaucrat, but do
you know how they measure Vision and Output? If their
Vision is about predictable quarterly numbers and positive
cash flow, and their Output is a stock price that makes all
your stock options valuable, are you sure you want to tell
them that all they are is paper pushers, and slow ones at
that? On the other hand, Finance, if you could streamline

your Processes so that the other organizations could get answers to financial questions more quickly, maybe those groups would be more productive and more innovative!"

Chris felt he was rolling now. "The point here is that you are all interdependent, and all have roles to play in a balanced, high performing enterprise. And the only way this works is for everyone to know their roles, know how others view their performance and all share a common view of what the corporate Vision, Process and Output goals are, and what they need to do to contribute. Perhaps now is a good time to take a quick bio break. When we come back, let's work our way through each organization, discuss why each of you rated it the way you did, and what would need to change for you to rate it closer to a Success. It looks like we have a lot to talk about."

Chris stood and headed out the door toward the restroom. At the same time, the door to the one-way viewing room opened and out walked the headhunter. He flashed a discreet "thumbs up." Chris continued down the hall. If you'd been close enough to hear what he murmured under his breath, you'd have heard two words.

"Thanks, Henry."

About the Author

For over 20 years, Gerry Langeler has served as a Managing Director with OVP Venture Partners (OVP), the most experienced venture capital firm in the Pacific Northwest. OVP was formed in 1983, and raised seven venture capital funds, the most recent at $250 million. The firm focused on early-stage companies in clean tech, digital biology, and information technology. OVP backed over 125 startups and saw over 50 major liquidity events, including 25 IPOs and more than 30 acquisitions by public companies.

From 1981 to 1992, Gerry was co-founder of Mentor Graphics Corporation (NASDAQ: MENT) where he served as President. He helped lead Mentor to over $400 million in sales and $1 billion in market capitalization. The company remains the fastest growing public software company to $200 million (in constant dollars) in US history. Now at over $1 billion in revenues, Mentor ranks as the second largest software company in the Pacific Northwest, behind only Microsoft.

His prior experience includes stints at Tektronix and

six years in the US Air Force Reserves.

Gerry's service as a board member includes digital media, energy, enterprise software, network security, wireless communications and biotechnology. He was appointed by Oregon's Governor to the Oregon Growth Board, where he serves as Co-chair. He was elected to and served as School Board Chair of the Riverdale Public School District. He previously served as Chair of the Riverdale School Foundation, Chair of the Oregon Museum of Science & Industry (OMSI) Board of Trustees, and Chair of the State of Oregon Facilities Authority, a bonding agency for not-for-profits. In 2011, he was awarded the Oregon Entrepreneurs Network Lifetime Achievement Award.

Gerry holds a BA in Chemistry from Cornell University and a MBA from Harvard University.

More at *www.langeler.com.*

Related Titles from Logos Press®

http://www.logos-press.com

Building Biotechnology
Scientists know science; businesspeople know business. This book explains both.
Yali Friedman

Hardcover ISBN: 978-1-934899-29-8
Softcover ISBN: 978-1-934899-28-1

Great Patents
Advanced Strategies for Innovative Growth Companies
David Orange, Editor

Softcover: 978-1-934899-18-2
Hardcover: 978-1-934899-17-5

Biotechnology Entrepreneurship
From Science to Solutions
Michael Salgaller, Editor

Hardcover ISBN: 978-1-934899-13-7
Softcover ISBN: 978-1-934899-14-4

CPSIA information can be obtained at www.ICGtesting.com
Printed in the USA
LVOW06s0752130314

377243LV00003B/89/P